Teaching Your
Child Concentration

A **PLAYSKOOL** Guide

Teaching Your Child Concentration

Lee Hausner, Ph.D.
Jeremy Schlosberg

LifeLine
Press
Washington, D.C.

Library of Congress Cataloging-in-Publication Data

Hausner, Lee.
    Teaching your child concentration: a Playskool® guide / Lee Hausner, Jeremy Schlosberg.
       p.   cm.
    Includes index.
    ISBN 0-89526-394-7 (pbk. : alk. paper)
    1. Attention—Study and teaching (Preschool)   2. Education, Preschool—Activity programs.   3. Education, Preschool—Parent participation. I. Schlosberg, Jeremy, 1958– . II. Title.
LB1065.H34 1998
370.15'3—dc21   98-12115
                                                          CIP

Published in the United States by
LifeLine Press
An Eagle Publishing Company
One Massachusetts Avenue, NW
Washington, DC 20001

Distributed to the trade by
National Book Network
4720-A Boston Way
Lanham, MD 20706

PLAYSKOOL® is a trademark of Hasbro, Inc.
© 1998 Hasbro, Inc.
All rights reserved.

Printed on acid-free paper.
Manufactured in the United States of America

10 9 8 7 6 5 4 3 2

Books are available in quantity for promotional or premium use. Write to LifeLine Press, One Massachusetts Avenue, NW, Washington, DC 20001, for information on discounts and terms or call (202) 216-0600.

Contents

PART THREE – Concentration: Building Block for Success and Happiness

Foreword

As the makers of Playskool® products, we recognize that the ability to concentrate is one of the most important skills a parent can foster, since concentration is the key to learning and intelligence.

And concentration is as essential today as it ever was—and perhaps even more critical now, since our children must cope with the frantic pace of modern life, the constant din of our media-dominated age.

You, the parent, can help. As the makers of Playskool® products, we strive to create tools that can help children develop their concentrational skills, but these, of course, are only tools. Teachers, friends, family, and even the media play important roles in fostering a child's concentration. But it is the parent who plays the biggest part in a child's development. By encouraging and collaborating with your child, you can immeasurably enhance your child's ability to concentrate.

We encourage you to take the steps now to set your child on the correct path to learning and growth. It is fun, and you will greatly improve your child's chances for leading a fulfilling and successful life.

Margaret C. Whitman
General Manager, Playskool®

PART ONE

The Importance of Concentration

CHAPTER ONE

The Gift of Concentration

Concentration seems like an old-fashioned idea in this trend-happy, web-surfing, time-pressured world of ours. Everything proceeds at breakneck speed: the sound bites that make up our news, the rapid-fire editing of our movies, the stream of data flowing through our computers. It's hard to know which came first, the frantic pace of the world that rushes past our eyes and ears, or our urgent need to be quickly informed and entertained.

For better or worse, this is the world in which our children have been raised—concentration is such an outdated skill! Our hectic and hurried lives discourage the act of focusing attention; the glut of information available on television and the onslaught of data from websites and Internet connections also give us the impression that we *need* to be constantly entertained, rapidly informed, and frequently updated.

If something doesn't grab our interest right away, we sit, with finger poised above the TV remote or the computer mouse, ready to click a program or screen into oblivion in the hope that the next one will satisfactorily occupy us for a few minutes.

Turn the television off and read a book? Seldom. Have a family discussion at dinner about current events? Hardly. The television is blaring our favorite sitcom, which we wouldn't want to miss. Okay, so how about watching it and then turning it off to discuss ideas or themes presented during the show that relate to our family? Nope. Either the program was too shallow, or it's time for another show. And so the evening goes.

> Concentration is at the very heart of learning and intelligence.

Is concentration becoming outdated? Have short attention spans become the norm? Sometimes it's easy to believe, when so many television shows seem geared toward short attention spans and seem to identify distraction as a positive and fun experience. Talk about encouragement!

The truth is that concentration is not any more outdated than learning. In fact, as long as we need to learn, we will need to concentrate because concentration is at the very heart of learning.

Why do we need concentration? Because our brains are limited. We can process only so much information at a single time. If we couldn't select and concentrate on one thing at a time, and stick with it long enough, we could never learn or even think. We must select and focus. One of the most powerful functions of concentration is actually to suppress thoughts—thoughts we don't need right now, that would get in the way of whatever it is we are doing, whether it's crossing the street or working out a new theory of physics. Without that suppression ability, our minds would be a jumble of random events, incapable of even simple cognitive processes.

Concentration is so important that it has been called a fundamental prerequisite of intelligence and has even been equated with intelligence itself.

Concentration, focusing the mind, is essential to *perceiving* what is going on around us and sifting that information for what is important and relevant. It helps us grasp, for instance, that the car horn we just heard is probably a more important piece of information than the leaf that just fell from that tree.

Concentration is essential to *comprehending* what we are reading or hearing. For instance, concentration helps us take special note when essential information is coming along, perhaps because we have seen a key word in the text, or because something is underlined, or because the teacher has changed her tone of voice. Children or even adults with poor concentration may even miss such obvious "cues," and they have a very hard time with subtle ones.

And concentration is absolutely essential to the formation of *memory*. What we pay attention to is what we tend to remember, especially if we comprehend its importance and can link it to other memories. Concentration is also essential to the later recall and use of those memories.

From the first moments of life, a baby begins to learn—and concentration is the tool she uses. But the newborn's ability to concentrate is limited and primitive. The ability to concentrate develops over time—or at least it should. That development is not automatic. We can help it along, or we can hinder it, with powerful results for the child's whole life.

A child who excels in concentration will probably excel in learning, in school, and in life. A child who concentrates poorly will have a hard time not only intellectually—in school and later—but even emotionally, because the frustrations that result from poor concentration and poor learning ability can make a child's social and personal life very painful. Substantial documentation shows that people who, as children, had difficulty concentrating in school not only tended to have a harder time in their careers, but even had some greater likelihood of getting into trouble with the law. Those are extreme cases, and you should not be frightened just because your four-year-old is fidgety. All four-year-olds are fidgety. But the fact remains that concentration is essential.

> Here is the good news: Concentration can be taught.

Are the frantic pace of modern life and the stimulation of the New Media affecting our children? It's hard to believe they aren't, though the precise effect is not always clear. Studies show that our children are not only declining academically, but also have some serious deficiencies in attention spans. Take young Teddy, for example. By age four he had already been described by various preschool teachers as temperamental, uncooperative, immature, and overactive. And those evaluations haven't changed much during kindergarten, except that now his teachers have added the phrase, "Doesn't live up to his potential."

It's hard for Teddy to sit still during story hour. He rarely completes a project, starting one and then shifting his attention to something else, working on it for a while, and then off again to something else. When Teddy does get involved in a project that interests him, he will often throw a tantrum when the teacher or his mother suggests it's time to do something else. Minor changes in his schedule also upset him and lead to more tantrums. When asked about his behavior, his parents sigh and say simply, "Teddy is not an easy child to raise."

Except on rare occasions, Teddy has trouble concentrating and is easily distracted. Is he simply a slow developer, exhibiting the flightiness typical of younger children? Is he, perhaps, bored with traditional classroom material? Does he have a different style of learning from his classmates? Or, does Teddy have what has come to be known as Attention Deficit Disorder (ADD)?

American children are twenty times more likely than children in other developed countries to be diagnosed as hyperactive or with ADD. In this country many of these children are treated with drugs, most notably Ritalin. We are also far more likely than other countries to diagnose slow, difficult, or flighty children as learning disabled.

Certainly some cases of ADD or learning disability have a deep organic or psychological cause. But it seems possible that for many children the problem of not being able to concentrate results from the overwhelming distractions of American culture. Many point to the endless entertainment of video games and TV, but children see this behavior mirrored in parents who come home from work only to "veg out" in front of the television. Clearly, it's not just television, but also the frenetic pace of our lives, the need for instant gratification, and an ineffectual and overburdened educational system, among other things, that contribute to our children's inability to concentrate.

But here is the really important truth: Concentration can be taught. If our children are not learning to concentrate, in most cases it is because something in our society, culture, or educational system is getting in the way.

The solution? Simple. Teach them.

Learning to concentrate means learning to learn. If we don't train our children to concentrate, they will never become good learners.

ADD diagnoses are running rampant in the United States; one expert claims it has reached "epidemic proportions." Clearly, concentration is a valuable trait to nurture in children, but as a society we are not doing it and in fact may be discouraging it. The book you're holding is one step toward teaching your child valuable concentration skills she will use for the rest of her life. Besides the activities described here, try "practicing what you preach" by reading instead of "zoning out" in front of the TV, becoming engaged in meaningful conversation, and taking pro-active steps to learn new and challenging things. Leading by example can set children on the right path early in life.

If you doubt that a child's ability to concentrate can be improved by training, think about babies. Babies are *born* with short attention spans. The ability to concentrate, to learn through focused attention and remembering, is one of the most important abilities they *acquire* as their nervous systems and brains develop. And as parents and educators we can—and should—encourage proper development of that ability.

How? Well, after the unconditional love of parents, probably the single most important development "tool" for infants and children is play. Play—the right kind of play—is the great teacher, and not just for human children. Virtually all mammals, and many other species, play, not just because it's fun, but also because play is essential to physical, intellectual, and emotional growth.

That's what this book is about. With a variety of games and activities, it will teach you how to help your child develop concentration. You will learn simple techniques for all ages that will help your child, over time, develop good concentration skills. As a matter of fact, as a good parent you've probably already begun to teach concentration without even realizing it....

Remember those days when, even before your infant could speak, she took the utmost delight in tossing a toy out of her crib? Dutiful parent that you are, you picked it up, so she could throw it again. And again, until long after you had first become delighted in her agility, your back had begun to complain, and you had begun to hope your baby would be *distracted* from this particular game. But did you also congratulate yourself on helping your infant develop her powers of concentration? Probably not. But that's exactly what you were doing. You were rewarding the child for staying focused on the toy even after she could not see it anymore. You were signaling to the child that it is good to pursue an activity over time. And by continuing to participate in the activity yourself you were giving an example of persistence and practicing something psychologists

> The games in this book build on children's naturally developing concentrational skills.

call "shared focus" (concentrating on something *with* your child), which is known to build her ability to concentrate.

Almost from the moment of birth, babies have some ability to focus their eyes. We can see this in the infant who gazes intently at the face of the person holding her, as if to fix that all-important person in her mind. This gaze is the "baby beginning" of the ability to concentrate.

Actually, the ears at first do a better job of focusing. A baby can distinguish voices before faces. Within three days, a newborn can tell whether a speaker is her mother or not and will demonstrate a preference for the mother's voice. By the time the baby is two weeks old, she will be able not only to distinguish between her father's voice and that of another male, but also to prefer her father's voice.

As her eyesight improves, she will come to distinguish mother's face from a stranger's. If she sees her mother's face but hears a stranger's voice, or sees a stranger's face while her mother is speaking, the baby will look away. This suggests that

Is Concentration at the Heart of Love, Power, and Financial Success?

Ever since William Shakespeare called lack of concentration "the disease of not listening, the malady of not marking," a number of famous writers have considered the influence of concentration—or the lack of it—on happiness, lovesickness, and the consequences of social actions.

Seventeenth-century French philosopher Nicolas de Malebranche considered the "attention of the intellect" to be a "natural prayer by which we obtain the enlightenment of reason."

But most of us can be thankful that the motivation for concentration doesn't always have to be so dramatic or conditional as English critic and conversationalist Samuel Johnson believed when he categorically stated that nothing concentrates the mind so wonderfully as when a man knows he is to be hanged in a fortnight.

If the need to achieve enlightenment and anxiety about death motivate us to concentrate, apparently so does being in love, according to the poet John Keats, who equated it with the intensity of feeling many of us have experienced when we are separated from our new love. "Every hour I am more and more concentrated in you; every thing else tastes like chaff in my mouth."

Attaching almost mythical importance to concentration, Ralph Waldo Emerson, the renowned nineteenth-century essayist and poet, called it the "secret of strength in politics, in war, in trade, in short in all management of human affairs." Twentieth-century Austrian writer Stefan Zweig, best known for his psychoanalytic biographies, echoed Emerson's sentiments when he called concentration "the eternal secret... of every mortal achievement."

Finally, the ever-practical Elbert Hubbard, American writer, editor, and publisher, who went down with the Lusitania, spoke of the importance of "concentration of the mind on whatever will ultimately put something in the pocket." Sounds like good advice for any era.

she can already make a clear association of the correct voice with the proper face.

Mother's face. Daddy's voice. These are among the first things any child learns, and she learns them the same way she learns so many things in life: by focused observation leading to firmly implanted memory. As with most things we learn, the process is not a conscious one. The baby does not think "focus" or "memorize" any more than she will do so later when learning language.

But as children continue to develop and grow, this instinctive focusing of attention on the characteristics, actions, and behaviors of others in the family—as well as other people—is crucial to their development. After all, much of what children learn can be acquired only by observation or imitation. This sort of learning feeds into what British psychologist Alan Baddeley calls a "script," which can be thought of as an integrated package of social information upon which children draw to interpret or understand a given event or situation. For instance, telling your child that you are going out to a restaurant evokes a "restaurant script" in her mind, which contains all the information the growing child has about restaurants.

Children naturally put enormous effort into this kind of learning. The energy they devote to observation and concentration makes them great mimics. When we find them displaying an embarrassing habit of ours, we may wish our children weren't able to concentrate quite so well! Yet research shows that this same ability—which you can encourage—will serve school-aged children well, resulting in higher achievement.

Concentration is in part a built-in skill, which is why all babies have some ability to concentrate from birth. But that doesn't mean we can't improve and build on that ability. If you think about it, almost all our abilities—from breathing to dancing to computer programming—are "built-in" to some extent.

And yet all of them can be improved through training. Even breathing—just ask a marathon runner!

An Amazing Journey

Everything begins with the brain, of course, and a child's ability to concentrate expands as the brain develops. There are many feats of concentration—and types of concentration—that will be impossible for kids until their nervous systems have grown to a certain level of maturity. Once the brain hits the right level of maturity, however, the ability to concentrate is learned first and foremost through experience and with practice.

So let's begin. First we will look a little bit at how a child's brain develops, helping us to understand better how and when to assist in that development. Then we will take a closer look at what concentration truly is, and how to foster it, because this will give you a better understanding of how the games and exercises work and how they will help you help your child.

Then we get to the fun part, an extensive selection of hands-on games and activities, grouped according to type of activity and age- or grade-appropriateness, all designed to help foster concentration.

After the games we have a few more important topics to discuss, including the influence of television and video games and our current school system, as well as some guidelines on the topic of ADD.

Remember: You can do it. In fact, you already do it—teach concentration, that is—naturally, by instinct, just as your child learns it. We're just going to help you both do it a little better, using play, the most natural learning tool ever created. Have fun!

CHAPTER TWO

Your Developing Child

You just had a baby! And there's your beautiful, sleepy newborn, with all five tiny fingers encircling just one of your own. Already your infant is beginning a lifetime experience of human sensations. Get ready, for you have unleashed a "learning vortex" with a built-in need to suck in mental activity.

At the source of that vortex is a complex brain, which authors Robert Ornstein and Richard Thompson liken to a "ramshackle house" that has been added onto over the years. Okay, not a very flattering way to think of your new baby, but understand that the difference in potential between your baby's brain and those of, say, your cat's cuddly kittens lies precisely in the size and potential for development of her "ramshackle" model.

Consider this: A kitten comes into the world with a brain that already has almost reached its full size and capacity for experience. While your baby's brain at birth is developed enough that she is sensitive to touch, pain, and changes in bodily position, her sensory and intellectual skills will continue to develop for years, even decades—possibly through her entire lifetime.

Your baby's brain will grow and develop, and the way she is nurtured, stimulated, and educated can alter how she develops—for better or for worse.

As life experiences provide stimulation, the newborn's brain—at first only 25 percent of its adult weight—will continue to increase in size. By the time a child is six years old, the brain is about the size of a grapefruit and almost identical to that of an adult. By the age of twelve, the child's nervous system and brain, which now weighs about as much as a head of cabbage, will have progressed from a place of largely reflexive actions (remember those grasping fingers?) to the point at which she can engage in abstract thinking.

> **Playing with your child is so critical because children learn through experimentation and training.**

Your newborn's complex brain and nervous system allow her to see, smell, and (as soon as the amniotic fluid is gone from the middle ear) hear right at birth. She can distinguish between salt and sugar, probably preferring the latter. Within the first two weeks of life, she can distinguish between a target in the form of a bull's-eye (her preference) and a blank circle. By one month, she can distinguish between a face and a nonface, preferring the face.

Your child begins to acquire the knowledge that is stored in her brain by concentrating, instinctively, on objects, activities, or interactions around her. During the first year of life, *motion* is one of the central qualities that prompts alertness and concentration in the infant. Movement of objects, sudden touches, and pulsing sounds will all hold her attention and allow her gradually to develop a variety of what are known as "schematic representations"—memories of the past that she can compare to present information in order to consider the differences.

To develop concentration, a newborn needs this ongoing neurological stimulation. A swinging mobile or bouncing toy will constantly make an impression in her tiny brain—inputting, inputting, inputting with each repetition. Even at this young age, your infant can easily get fixated on a moving object for thirty seconds or so, until something else—a noise, another toy—distracts her.

By two months, cognitive and memory processes have begun. At this age, your bright and perceptive infant can detect the difference between a striped pattern and a completely gray one, as well as between linear and curved lines. She is especially interested in the colors red and orange. And she can discriminate between the musical notes C and C sharp. (You may not even be sure that you can do this!)

At three months, she enjoys looking at her own hands, and can distinguish her mother's face from that of a stranger. By four months, your growing baby can tell the difference between happy and sad faces, although she is unable to comprehend the emotion behind the different faces.

Somewhere around the seven-month mark, her concentration and attention abilities have developed to the point at which she begins to notice details and can play alone or entertain herself for short periods of time. Around eight months, she begins to imitate others, to hold two toys and examine them, and to try to obtain toys that are out of her reach. By eleven months, many things hold her interest and attention, especially toys and people. These simple acts of grasping and glancing are the beginnings of intelligence.

All of these advances are the result of brain growth. And yet at the same time, the brain is also busy eliminating certain neurological "circuits" that were laid down during the months in

Is TV the Enemy?

Your child's attention is so fixed on his favorite television show that you can't get his attention. Is he too "concentrated" on the show to respond? If you've noticed that your child's intense ability to focus doesn't carry over into homework or chores, congratulate yourself on being an alert and perceptive parent. It's precisely because television is what it is—lively, vivid, and quick-moving—that it does not promote real concentration.

Because it jumps from image to image, television neither encourages nor allows time for the viewing child to stop and think about the ideas presented, or to inspire him to imagine or figure out the consequences of certain actions for himself. Before your child has time to activate his own thinking and focusing processes, there's another image on the screen, and then another.

Surveys report that kids watch television twenty-five to fifty-four hours per week, more hours than many spend in school. So, of course, TV has an undeniable influence on your child. But does it greatly affect how well your child can concentrate? Well, there is extensive debate on this subject (as you will see in Chapter 8), but many researchers warn that TV can have an adverse affect on concentration. For instance, psychiatrist Matthew Dumont suggests that television's whizbang pace—its "incessant changes of camera and focus," which cause viewers to shift reference points every few seconds—may actually program and encourage the development of short attention spans. Another expert calls TV watching "zombie viewing."

This may be scary to parents who consider the television a semi-educational baby-sitter. In fact, even most advocates *for* the value of television urge parents to be watchful of content and to limit viewing time. So, maybe placing a sketch pad, journal, science book, or baseball glove in your child's hand would be a better solution.

the womb. This process results in the growing child's ability to inhibit certain generic, automatic reactions and to develop more specific and conscious ones. In essence, intellect begins to eclipse instinct as your child's brain learns and grows. Concentration "feeds" the growing, hungry brain by delivering as much information as possible. By learning to concentrate better, a child stays focused enough to maximize the amount of data being sent; hence, a stimulating environment really does give your brain "food" for thought!

As the "automatic" circuits are shut down, new circuits that become the basis of learning are established. This is true not only for humans but also for many other species with relatively advanced brains, i.e., brains that function by learning as well as instinct. In one famous experiment the brains of rats who lived alone in their cages, with no toys and nothing to do all day, were compared to the brains of rats who lived in groups and who could play with lots of toys, wheels, a ball, and so on. The rats who had something to do developed more—and more complex—brain circuitry.

> The key is developing the ability to concentrate for longer and longer periods of time.

Neurological connections in one side of the brain or the other become slightly stronger depending on outside stimulation and the use of either the right or left side of the body. Experts assert that a lack of exterior stimulation during these early months can seriously and negatively affect the growth of a child's brain and nervous system. It's not that a large part of the newborn's brain isn't physiologically formed at birth; it certainly is. But many of the nerves involved in higher mental processes are still immature—they need the training and input that only concentration delivers in order to reach full capacity and maturity.

Concentration is so important to your child because it is the only way to create a neurological pattern in the brain. These neurological pathways are what constitute memory, abstract thinking, and higher-level thought processes. The only way of developing and enhancing these pathways is through repetition and paying attention. For example, if you shoot one thousand basketballs every day, you are training your mind and body in that neurological activity pattern. You may never become Michael Jordan, but you will have trained your brain to perform this task quickly and efficiently by using your powers of concentration. Undoubtedly you will sink more baskets than someone who shoots once a month.

So, by engaging your child in diverse, challenging, and stimulating activities (like our games in Chapters 4 through 7), you are training different neurological pathways. Although each pathway may not be used right away, think of it as training for later in life, or exercise for the mind. Essentially, by focusing on different activities involving all sorts of concentration skills, the brain is learning how to learn.

Okay, that's a neurological simplification of what goes on in the brain. And child development is not reducible to neurology. Psychology has also made crucial contributions to understanding what happens developmentally as your child's ability to concentrate evolves.

Swiss child psychologist Jean Piaget conducted some of the earliest and most incisive studies on how children learn and develop memory. Piaget believed that learning was a structured and organized process that occurs as new experiences overlay and combine with prior knowledge. Of course, Piaget is not the only psychologist of note on this topic, but his groundbreaking research has profoundly influenced our understanding of child development.

According to Piaget, a child's intellectual development occurs in four different chronological stages characterized by qualitatively different forms of thought. There is no clear or abrupt change or distinction between one stage and the next; children pass through them in a slowly integrated manner. Moreover, learning theoreticians have discovered that children can develop and learn things even earlier than Piaget thought. During all these periods, a child's major source of new knowledge and learning comes first by experimentation, followed by training. That's precisely why active steps, like the games and activities included in this book, are so crucial, even at a young age. This type of concentration training can capitalize on your child's expanding con-

> Developing concentration early accelerates the learning process and increases your child's chances for life success.

sciousness and can greatly impact your child's success later in life.

In Piaget's scheme of cognitive development, sensorimotor development dominates infant growth during the first two years. Children learn to manipulate objects, to move about, and to initiate events. Their perception and memory begin to be organized, but they have neither much curiosity regarding results, nor the notion of retaining the knowledge of results. As one writer put it, a two-year-old may love helping mommy wipe off the kitchen table, but she won't care very much if it is clean when she is done. She loves the physical process.

During this time the infant acquires some of her early competence through what Harvard psychologist Jerome Bruner calls "mastery play." For example, your six-month-old child first notices a new object, reaches for it, grabs it, and puts it into her mouth. She is fully concentrating on the object and therefore gains her first understanding of the object. To understand it more fully, she may then shake it, bang it on something nearby,

Television or Books?
Mindlessness versus Personal Empowerment

For the umpteenth time, you read your child her favorite story. It's an intimate, nonrambunctious time, but most importantly (and you may not even realize it), you've begun to teach your child how to listen and pay attention. You've begun to empower your child with the knowledge that quiet times are important and special. Soon the stories and the time together grow longer as your child naturally develops the ability to concentrate for longer periods of time, and, as language develops, the two of you can talk about the story.

Reading has a number of advantages over television for promoting concentration. By its very nature, reading—and especially reading aloud—allows you and your child to control the pace at which information is received and understood. You can stop and reread something you didn't quite understand the first time, or talk about feelings a story or poem arouses. Your children are learning to recognize their own needs to review material or to go to another source for more information. They're developing the ability to ponder the implications and consequences of certain actions, to think clearly and analytically, and to listen to their own inner stirrings.

When you read yourself, and read to your children, you are modeling a basic way to sustain concentration. By going to the library for books and taking books along during both short and long trips, you demonstrate that books, unlike television, are easily accessible and transportable. Your child learns she is in control; she doesn't have to allow television to dictate when and where she will be entertained or enlightened.

Television is largely a one-way street, passively seducing your child with its own images. Books, on the other hand, are ever-available and actively engross your child's mind and send her along a two-way street. They help her to concentrate and develop her own imaginative abilities—to evaluate her life, her wishes, and her fears.

throw it down, and otherwise engage in activities that tell her more about this particular object. And, as we learned earlier, her body is busy sending neuronal messages to the brain. Granted, this is not a very complex type of learning, but by the time your child is ready to learn something like algebra, she will have acquired the building blocks of concentration, discovery, and learning that will help her pay attention and avoid distraction while listening to her math teacher. That's why early tactile stimulation—having lots of interesting, colorful (and safe!) objects within reach to explore is so important for child development.

Sometime around fifteen to twenty-four months, the child increases her concentrational ability to persevere in short goals and to know when she has achieved them. This is often signified by the child's smiling to herself without needing to look at an adult for confirmation—what another Harvard psychologist, Jerome Kagan, calls a "private, not social" smile. This is significant because it indicates a blossoming interior life and the child's growing sense of satisfaction and contentment. By focusing her attention on something (a hard-to-hold fork) the child learns to savor the rewards of concentration, and thus smiles and coos happily as she eats. Repeated success, parental encouragement, and the resulting increased confidence are fundamental to developing concentration, especially the ability to stick with a task. Frustration leads to withdrawal and refusal to try new things—a developmental disaster.

From ages two to seven, children begin to activate their sensorimotor abilities themselves and to have more control over them. Now they are not just inputting and processing random information, but they are also interacting more with their environment and developing more mature concentration skills. Language development begins, and children become able to create internal representations of their world, albeit a totally egocen-

tric one. Age five is the ideal time for children to begin more
multifaceted concentration training games, because all their
cognitive, verbal, and sensorimotor developments are near
completion, and more complex scenarios, rules, and higher-
level thinking can be employed.

During the period between ages seven and eleven, children
develop the ability to form concrete ideas and to apply logic to
them. Concepts such as length, mass, and volume become sta-
ble and can be applied to various situations. They can also
attend to activities that don't require as much sensory input—
spending more time on a jigsaw puzzle, dollhouse, or epic fan-
tasy novel.

Sometime around eleven or twelve years and onward, our
children enter the period in which adult powers of reasoning,
abstraction, and symbolization gradually emerge. These higher-
level processes were developed by the concentrational abilities
learned earlier in life. In addition, social interactions and mores
become clear and, often to our dismay, youths begin to pick and
choose those they think are right or usable.

The Child-Rearing Challenge

The key to raising attentive children is lengthening the time
your child can concentrate within an appropriate range. As
we've discussed, the actual ability to concentrate is instinc-
tual—any child will concentrate on something put in front of
her. So the real challenge is developing the ability to concentrate
and tune out distraction for longer and longer periods of time.
As your child advances through school and the material gets
more and more complex, she must be able to concentrate for a
sustained period of time, no matter how boring that college lecture might be. The games and activities in this book are giving

you a head start. By beginning the process of developing concentration early, you're accelerating the learning process and offering your child an important component of life success.

Some caveats: Since individual cognitive abilities mature at different rates in different children, it is important while employing the activities in this book that you respect your child's ability and maturity level. Keep in mind that many younger children can hold only a couple of things in their heads at once. They can pay attention to the two instructions they heard, and can succeed at those tasks, but they cannot concentrate on a huge laundry list of directives. So telling a child to use the bathroom, tie her shoes, get her jacket and bookbag, and wait by the door so she's ready for the carpool in ten minutes can be a confusing, overwhelming experience for her. When she's still tying her shoes, you may get angry and say: "I just

Motoring Along

The development of fine motor coordination—itself a form of concentration—is an important milestone for children, and has been linked by researchers to academic performance in school. Especially in the early grades, children who are most dexterous appear to have a marked advantage over less-developed students. This is true, say the experts, because children with more developed fine motor skills can reproduce what they see and imagine without bogging themselves down in the physical process of it. Not only do these children feel more free to follow their imaginations, but also their ability to get written work done quickly and accurately reinforces their developing attention spans. This, in turn, leads to continued classroom success, increased self-motivation, and even better concentration skills.

told you to get ready, weren't you paying attention?" This, obviously, has ramifications for her self-image. And guess what? It doesn't help her concentrate any better in the future.

Certainly you've been in church or at some other formal service and seen a young child who just couldn't sit still—a four-year-old squirming in her seat, looking around, tapping her shoes together. And what did you think when you saw this? You probably thought, "What an ill-tempered brat" or "Why can't she behave?" Right? Well, her behavior certainly wasn't bratty, but was entirely appropriate to a four-year-old—even one schooled in manners. Now, if the child was screaming, running up and down the aisles, and pulling off her mother's hat, that would be inappropriate. So remember—don't impose adult standards for concentration, endurance, or etiquette on your child. An attentive, polite child can be well behaved, but there are limits because of age.

As maturation occurs and experience builds, your child will gradually be able to move on to greater feats of concentration. At whatever level your child succeeds, she needs encouragement and praise in order to think of herself as capable. Your encouragement is an important motivation for your child to continue active approaches to concentration. Be aware, too, that parents are often not the best judges of age appropriateness, achievement, and ability levels because they tend to view their own child subjectively and want her to excel.

Also important to know is when to back off and let children grasp concepts and focus their attention of their own accord. Research shows, for instance, that at a young age, concentration is best fostered by a parent's encouraging independence and not overly directing. Those "terrible" two-year-olds get quite upset when they are unable to meet a standard for mastery set or imposed by an adult. But they'll feel immense satisfaction if they accomplish a task with minimal guidance from a parent.

At all ages, children need time and the opportunity to explore and learn on their own, to experiment and watch what happens for however long it takes. Rushing in to help a child before she has asked for assistance ties the child to the parent. This doesn't mean you should leave your child unsupervised; it does mean that as a parent, you can begin to learn a few basic behaviors that provide the foundation for a household in which concentration becomes a valued skill.

We'll go into all of this in more detail, but here are some of the basic tenets of improving concentration in your child:

※ ENCOURAGE rather than discourage;

※ PROTECT from interruption;

※ COLLABORATE rather than control.

Encourage your child's natural inclination to concentrate on tasks particularly interesting to her, and show her that putting in time and effort is an acceptable—and even desirable—way of behaving.

Finally, and we can't stress this last idea enough: Pressure to succeed is futile. Everybody got that? *Pressure to succeed is futile.* Unless, perhaps, your goal is to foster neurosis. A subtle but important part of possessing good learning and concentration skills is a positive attitude, strengthened by confidence. Help your child become aware of all the ways she can concentrate and remember; don't focus on the ways she can't. Her developing concentrational abilities, coupled with your praise, will add immeasurably to your child's sense of self-esteem and self-confidence.

Improving Concentration

So how are we going to improve concentration?

First we need a clearer picture of what concentration is and how it works. We'll find that it has several different components or tasks, which we will define. It is by improving on each of those tasks that children, or even adults, can improve their concentration, which means improving their very ability to learn.

One word of caution. Concentration is one of the most important of all human abilities, an absolutely necessary tool for almost all our intellectual abilities... it is a veritable building block of the mind. But our knowledge of how the mind or the brain works is far from complete, and so therefore is our understanding of concentration. Yet we have learned a great deal in recent decades. And even though huge gaps in our knowledge remain, what we do know can help us understand what concentration is and how to improve it.

Do you remember what school was like, late in the spring, when summer vacation began to beckon? I still have vivid memories of my third grade year, particularly as spring warmed and stretched toward summer: My classmates and I got more and more wiggly—and more and more giggly—as each day brought us closer to the end of the school year. Our poor teacher, Miss Hershey, became a broken record. "Settle down now," she'd say. "Concentrate on your work," she'd implore. "Sit still," she would urge. "Pay attention," she demanded, again and again.

"Pay attention!" Concentration means paying attention. Some dictionaries even define concentration as "direction of attention to a single object." And if you look in most child psychology books, you won't find the word "concentration" in the index. Psychologists today usually refer to what we call concentration as "attention," "attention span," or "ability to focus attention."

> **Why is it easier to concentrate on and learn somewhat difficult subjects than extremely easy ones?**

How important is that ability? Well, we could not use our minds without it. As one eminent scientist phrased it, concentration or attention "is the focus of consciousness," the process by which we select either from our current sensory input—sight, hearing, touch, and so on—or from our memory, the information we are going to use to solve a problem as complex as how to write a description of concentration or as simple as picking out a pair of 10s in a poker hand.

Here is a well-known piece of experimental research that helps make clear just how important this ability to "focus" concentration is: There are two groups of children. The first group consists of proficient learners and problem solvers who do very well in school. In the second group are students who are not nearly so proficient and who have trouble in school. Both groups are given a test in which they are required to perform two tasks *at the same time,* a "primary" task and a "secondary" task. The primary task might be reading a short passage and answering some questions on the contents. The secondary task—which they try to do while they are reading—might be listening to the teacher recite random numbers and raising their hands whenever the teacher says the same number twice in a row.

Who does better? Well, as you probably guessed, the good learners do better on the primary task. But here is the surprise. The poor learners beat the good learners on the secondary task. Why? Not because the poor learners are better at knowing when two numbers match. When that is the *only* task, the good learners do better on that, also. The reason the poor learners do better at the secondary task is because they are *not* good at concentrating. The good learners concentrate so forcefully on the main job of reading the passage that they can barely hear what the teacher is saying. But the poor learners are easily distracted from the main job so they do hear what the teacher is saying and actually do better at the secondary task.

How does concentration work? That is far from clear, but we do understand enough to help us and our children become better at it.

To start, we know that we can tell our minds to concentrate—though our minds don't always cooperate. Much concentration is automatic—which is why we jump when we hear a car horn even though a split second before we were not thinking to ourselves, "Listen for car horns; they mean danger." But most concentration is the result of a deliberate effort. When Miss Hershey said "pay attention," we knew what she was talking about. We have "attention resources," and within limits we can decide to "pay" or allocate them in a particular direction. The better we become at this, the better we are at concentrating, and the better we will be at learning (forming memory) and problem solving.

One thing we have confirmed (although in a way we've known it for thousands of years) is that it is actually easier to concentrate on and learn somewhat difficult subjects than extremely easy ones. Sound bizarre? Well think of a challenging subject that you know something about, but is not totally overwhelming. A new wrinkle in the tax laws for an accountant, a new legal precedent for a lawyer, a new piece of machinery for a machinist. Challenging subjects all. Now think of some numbers, say "4," "12," and "5." Easy.

The important new information about accounting or whatever is complicated, and there's lots of it. The numbers are simple and carry little information (outside the context of a mathematical problem). But for exactly that reason you would have an easier time paying attention to and later remembering the gist of an article or lecture on one of those challenging subjects than you would trying to listen to or remember a random series of one hundred numbers listed or read aloud. The individual numbers are so "easy," so lacking in meaning, that it seems our brain can't get a hold of them and lock them down. Memory experts who use mnemonic devices to remember things such as random lists of numbers actually succeed by making the list far *more complicated*, for instance by associating each number with another image in their minds. As a result, there is more information to be remembered, but in this case that turns out to be easier than remembering less.

Reading experiments show a similar result. When a good reader reads a passage of text made up of some important and challenging information that also has some not very informative, easy "fluff," they slow down for the important part, work harder at comprehending it, and remember it much better than the easy "fluff."

Why? As we saw in the previous chapter, the brain learns by establishing new sets of electrochemical circuits among its neurons as it takes in new information. Much like the charged or uncharged circuits of a computer, that circuitry seems to store the information. Not all the information that passes through our senses is recorded. The brain seems to make a "decision" to record certain information and build new circuits. Apparently (science here has a long way to go) the more circuits that are made or modified in reaction to a piece or pieces of information, the more likely we are to remember that information. And if the new information is easily related to old information for which circuits already exist, we are even more likely to build effective new circuits.

Random numbers don't relate to much; they have little meaning. ("Why are you reading me this meaningless string of numbers?") Less meaning may result in less circuit building, less to "tie" the memory to. Those complicated mnemonic devices may inspire more circuit building, making it possible to remember the numbers.

On the other hand, information that is extremely hard to understand can overwhelm us, making it impossible to pay attention. Once in college I took a very technical course for which I was unprepared. The lectures were literally meaningless to me, and I could not remember a single thing or even take usable notes. My better-prepared classmates told me the lectures were brilliant, ground-breaking stuff, but all I could think was "why is he spouting all this gibberish," right before I started daydreaming. To me those lectures were about as memorable as if the professor had spent hours reciting a string of random numbers.

Mnemonics: The Art of Memory

According to mythology, we have Mnemosyne (KNEE-mahs-eh-KNEE), the Greek goddess of memory and mother of the Muses, to thank for our memory abilities. From her name we derive the word "mnemonics" (the first m is silent), which refers to any strategy that helps us organize and remember information.

In the first century B.C., the Roman orator Cicero recounted the tale of the poet Simonides and history's earliest feat of amazing memorization. Around 500 B.C., a nobleman of Thessaly commissioned Simonides to chant a lyric poem at a banquet. The night of the celebration, the roof of the banquet hall fell in, crushing all the guests—except Simonides, who was outside at that time. By remembering the places where the guests had been sitting, Simonides was able to help relatives identify their dead. As a result of his ability, Simonides is considered the inventor of the art of memory.

Pondering his experience, Simonides devised the first visual imagery system of mnemonics. He would visualize a room (a "memory palace") and then "place" the various items he wanted to remember in special locations about the room. Whenever he needed to recall these items, he simply "looked" at the appropriate place in his mind's eye. Many of the visual mnemonic techniques used today are simply variants of Simonides' technique. Research shows, for instance, that the memory palace is a popular and effective technique for teaching foreign languages.

You can utilize some of these visualization techniques with your children, too. Ask them to close their eyes and describe Grandma's kitchen, or get really creative and describe pretend things like what's in Little Red Riding Hood's picnic basket. By focusing their attention, they can "see" things they wouldn't ordinarily see, and describing these items helps their verbal skills, too.

Remember this; it will be important later. Somewhat challenging material stimulates concentration and builds the mind. But material that is too challenging stifles concentration and leads to frustration, boredom, and giving up.

Sometimes concentrating feels like work. It is. Educational psychologists speak of "effortful" mental processes such as "sustained attention." These "efforts" can be conscious or unconscious, but extensive research suggests that it is during these times of great effort that the brain is learning and reasoning. And science has even found some evidence that we can measure when people are in a high attention state—for instance, by the slowing down of the heart beat.

Let's review for a moment. We know what concentration does: It is essential to learning and to forming memory. It is essential to recalling from memory the appropriate information we need to work on a problem. It is essential to reasoning and indeed to all thought, because if we could not focus the mind we would not be able to use it effectively. Researchers have observed that some children with severe ADD/hyperactivity, arising from an apparent brain defect, simply lack this "editing function." They literally cannot exclude irrelevant thoughts from their minds. But even the rest of us with only ordinary difficulties concentrating can have this same problem many times a day: When it happens we say we "lost our train of thought." We know we were thinking quite seriously about something important just a moment ago, but then another thought or event intruded and now we cannot even remember what we were thinking about. That is a lapse of concentration, a loss of attention.

And we know a bit about how concentration works: A good concentrator signals the brain, consciously or unconsciously, that certain information is important and needs to be retained or processed. This signal leads to the formation or modification of brain circuitry. It is easier to concentrate (and the brain is more likely to form useful circuitry) on information we can comprehend, on unusual and important information even when the important information is challenging, and on subjects about which we already have some circuitry in place. Random and meaningless information is hardest to focus on and thus hardest to form a memory of. And the more we use and are engaged by information, the more likely we are to focus on it and commit it to memory.

From all this we can see that concentration has several components or aspects. By understanding the different components of concentration we can understand what it is we are trying to teach and why the games and exercises in this book will help us help our children become better concentrators.

The Components of Concentration

Concentration has three basic components:

1) discrimination;

2) intensity; and

3) duration of effort, otherwise known as "attention span."

Some researchers list more or fewer, but they are really talking about these three. Let's look at the components in detail.

1. Discrimination is sometimes called "selection" or even "search" (though search is really a subset of discrimination). In a nutshell "discrimination" is the form of concentration that tells the brain what to concentrate on.

Here's an example: If a group of students are given questions ahead of time that can be answered by a passage of text they are about to read, they will focus on the parts of the text that answer the questions and pay less attention to the rest. That is discrimination, in this case helped along by powerful external "cues." Usually readers don't have such explicit cues; they have to find their own cues in the text. That is a somewhat more demanding discrimination task and an extremely important skill.

At whatever age and level of ability, good learners are marked by their superiority in being able to discover and attend to the appropriate cues not only in reading but also in any task; they have more efficient attentional skills than slower learners. Children who are quicker at zeroing in on the relevant cues are faster learners.

Fortunately, we know children can and do learn to be better at discrimination. We can help them with the right kind of training. Practice at reading and *studying* appropriately challenging types of material *can* make us better at discrimination almost automatically. But research has shown that helping children with cues will eventually make them better at finding cues on their own.

In the beginning or with a new task, children who are told explicitly which cues to watch for are able to concentrate and learn better. Younger children are too inexperienced and immature to develop their own strategies for finding cues independently. Being asked to do so without help or hints interferes with their concentration. From age nine on, however, children begin to be able to formulate their own strategies. Hyperactive children benefit more from strategy instructions or cues than nonhyperactive children.

Cues are not always verbal instructions. Sometimes a cue just means trying a similar but easier task first. The child achieves a rewarding success so she will be more willing to work a bit harder on the next task, and also picks up hints as to how to find the important information for this type of task.

For instance, in Chapter 7 we offer several variations of that old favorite game, Concentration. Well, it's close to impossible to ask most five- or six-year-olds to play Concentration with fifty-two cards. They will get frustrated and give up because they have too much information to handle. The "cue"—to try to remember where the unmatched cards are when you turn them back face down—is too hard to use with so many cards, and so will not be learned. In fact the "game" may end in tears, frustration, or sullen silence. But start the game with six cards (three pairs) or a dozen (six pairs), and she will learn. Soon you may be amazed to see your young child playing proficiently with an entire deck, a great aid in developing short-term memory and the two other aspects of concentration detailed below.

> Three keys to concentration: Practice, repeated success, and encouragement from parents and teachers.

Tactile cues often work better to help three- and four-year-old children concentrate on and correctly discriminate between objects. Not only is tactile learning an important and often neglected form of learning, but also practicing this form of discrimination clearly improves other forms later. In fact, we have a whole chapter of games devoted to tactile concentration.

How a child improves in such fundamental learning skills as reading is a profound subject, intimately tied up with the workings of the brain. A small army of educational psychologists and other scientists devote their professional lives to researching and debating such issues. But not every example of concentration involves such deep questions. Sometimes kids just need to learn sensible everyday hints and strategies, preferably through experience.

Think of that trick test you may have once gotten in grade school, when the teacher warned everyone to read all the questions on the test before starting. And one of the last questions informed you that it was not a real test and you didn't have to do it. Those children who didn't pay attention to the directions in the first place and just began the test did not succeed. They did not make sure to gather all the relevant information first. The kids who were fooled probably did not need to learn that lesson twice. This is also one you can help by example. At the holidays or on birthdays, before you start assembling the new favorite toy, *do* read the instructions!

2. Intensity of effort. We know that consciously trying to concentrate can increase learning (although under the wrong conditions, such as excessive pressure, it can actually do the opposite). Even when we are not conscious of the effort, it may be there working for us. Remember that turning on this effort is one of the things discrimination does for us. Discrimination gives the signal to turn up the heat, as "cued" readers do when they hit the important passages.

We know that, within certain limits, we learn better when we make things a bit harder for ourselves. To memorize a speech, for instance, it usually is not enough just to read it over and over. The words soon get so familiar that we stop paying attention to them, and no more or at least very little learning occurs. To really imprint the speech it works much better to rehearse saying the lines without looking at the page. (We can also use more efficient methods such as mnemonic devices). Harder tasks require more attention, and once we "pay" that attention we are more likely to learn and remember. Effort equals recall.

We also know that our capacity for mental effort, just like physical effort, is limited. And we know we can increase that capacity with practice. However, we don't understand nearly as well how brain "workouts" produce their effect as how muscle workouts achieve results.

Part of the reason we get better at this intense concentration with practice may have to do with the wiring of the brain. Practice may make us more efficient at setting up neural pathways. Or perhaps a brain with more working circuits has an easier time adding to the circuitry. But part of the effect is clearly conscious and psychological, even emotional. As we experience this intense state of concentration *and* we recognize that it produces the desired results, we become more willing to enter that state.

> Children learn better when they are interested; that's why play is the great teacher.

There are thus three keys here: Practice at tasks that are challenging but well within possibility; repeated success; and encouragement, especially from parents and teachers.

3. Duration of effort, or attention span, and persistence. Just as with discrimination, there are two sorts of issues here: Deep questions having to do with the functioning of the brain over time periods measured in seconds or minutes, and commonsense issues of good old-fashioned dedication and persistence over the course of hours, days, or years, even in the face of obstacles or difficulties. And yet the ways to improve both are very similar.

Let's take duration of effort, or basically the time spent in the intense concentration state while engaged in a particular learning task. The goal is simple: Longer is better. Repeated experiments show that very small increases in time—perhaps a few seconds, depending on the task—spent in intense concentration on a task can be the difference between learning or not. The ADD child's fidgeting, which may have him jumping from toy to toy or task to task at several times the rate of an average youngster, can be devastating not only to his learning of that particular task but also to his learning how to learn. But extensive research shows that this habit *can* be improved.

"Sticking with it" is so important that one expert has proclaimed simply, "Concentration *is* time on task." We don't go so far, but it is a big part of the picture.

How can we teach children to stick with it? As with intensity, practice and repeated success are key. But this is also a case in which our example and the way we interact with our children have a big impact. In short: They may develop longer attention spans if we give them a good example and if we sometimes concentrate with them. Episodes of "shared" attention—when parent and child are concentrating on the same thing or activity, or on each other—are invaluable.

Experiments have shown that children of parents who "fuss"—that is, who interrupt or join their children's activities uninvited—tend to have shorter attention spans. The problem is that parents who interrupt are "modeling" short attention spans to their children, and they are actually frustrating the children's attempts to concentrate.

So once again: practice, good example, and encouragement. For longer tasks—say, building a model racer or decorating a doll house—good concentration does not necessarily mean starting a task and sticking to it without interruption until it's done. Few important tasks in life can be handled that way. The ability to work for a while, leave for something else, and then

Coaxing Concentration:
How Actors Memorize Long Speeches

Memory works by making links between information. Using the three most important principles underlying memorization—association, imagination, and location—actors memorize their parts by creating and fitting facts into imaginatively created mental structures and frameworks. Using these same techniques, you can teach your child memory tricks she'll use and remember for the rest of her life.

Rhythm and movement are also helpful in memorization; that's why songs are easier to remember than speeches. To take advantage of this principle, some actors won't even begin to learn their lines until the movements of the scene are laid out. Once the actor knows where his various "ending locations" are, he uses them as a framework on which to "hang" parts of his presentation.

Actors also use a modification of the mnemonic technique devised by Simonides (see page 40). First, the actor breaks the performance down into key words, and then he creates images (imagination, once again) to remind him of each of the key words. After that, he takes a journey—long or short, depending on the amount of material to be remembered—through a familiar place, leaving each key-word image in one of the places along the route. To remember, he simply walks through the locale again.

So try these memorization and concentration tasks with your child. By identifying key phrases, just like actors, she can memorize such useful cultural touchstones as the Pledge of Allegiance, a bedtime or religious prayer, or the national anthem.

return again and again until the task is finished actually shows more impressive concentration.

Thus in teaching children to concentrate, it can be important to focus on *eventual* achievement rather than the behavioral style by which it was accomplished. Especially at younger ages, some kids just can't sit still as long as others. But this does not mean they are not concentrating; it absolutely does not mean that they are ADD kids; and it does not mean that they will not learn to stay at one task for a long time. To help them toward that day, however, it is valuable to focus on the idea of committing to a goal and persevering until it's finished, rather than artificially imposing a "don't do anything else until you're done" rule.

Long-term concentration is also related to some other attributes, notably planning, striving, and achievement. Psychologist David McClelland spent his career researching "achievement motivation," a skill that is learned and developed. When your child sets a goal she wants to accomplish, that's achievement motivation. When she plans what needs to be done to achieve the goal, does the work it takes, or overcomes the obstacles, that's one form of concentration. Some psychologists prefer to identify this complex, integrated process as "striving." Whatever you call it, concentration is an integral part of the achievement process.

These three characteristics—discrimination, intensity, and duration of effort—form the basis for concentration in adults. But notice the wonderful thing about all three of them: All are behaviors that can be easily encouraged, nurtured, and rewarded in children.

In fact, as we'll see, teaching your child concentration skills really involves three simple things:

1. Giving her lots of opportunities to practice and hone these three traits and turn them into habits. That's where the games and activities in this book come in.

2. Being very encouraging about all three of these components so she knows you approve, and so she associates these behaviors with exciting, rewarding times. This includes creating a home environment in which these three behaviors are practiced and valued by adults as well as children. It also means helping your child find activities that challenge her without overwhelming her. If the task is overwhelming, not only will she not learn anything, she also may actually learn harmful "lessons," like thinking is hard, and "I am no good at it," and "I am not going to get suckered into trying this again!"

Frustration is a huge enemy of concentration. How well do you concentrate when you are emotionally distraught or your stomach is in a knot? We know one mother who was convinced her son had ADD because he had a tendency to "throw a fit" within seconds of attempting a task that he immediately gave up on in frustration over what he perceived as instant failure. Sounds like ADD, right? The inability to stick out a project or even give it a good try; the emotion; bouncing off the walls. But it wasn't ADD. This kid was smart, but he had been given a task he wasn't capable of. In fact, it was always happening to him, for the simple reason that both the boy and the adults around him based their guess of what he should have been capable of on his mental abilities. Meanwhile his motor skills were developing more slowly. The child's life was a constant exercise in frustration because his brain had him taking on more than his body could handle. He was mad as heck. Then his body grew up, and he grew out of it.

3. Finally, and very important: Concentration is encouraged by interest. Reams of scientific data exist to prove even this apparently obvious point: Children learn better when they are interested. Whatever one thinks of her methods generally, Maria Montessori's great insight remains valid: Ultimately the child is her own best teacher because it is when she becomes passionately interested that she not only learns about her passion, but also learns how to learn.

How do you help a child find an interest? Encouraging her to explore a wide array of interests to which she can shift her attention when she becomes bored is a natural way to promote concentration. Even very young children can benefit from this. Confronted with a pile of colorful books, who knows which one the four-year-old will choose? But when she finds the one she wants you to read her ten times in a row, you know something is being awakened. One four-year-old of our acquaintance entered a "dinosaur phase" and started demanding every book published on the subject. Before he was through he was reading the books himself, though no one had ever taught him, and he was even helping grown-ups "sound out" the more difficult dinosaur names.

Interest and motivation: That's why we believe so strongly in using play as an educational tool. Kids love to play, and you will love watching them learn as they do. So let's begin.

PART TWO

Activities and Games

The following four chapters contain games and activities that will help children hone their concentration in simple—and *fun*—ways.

As you will see, the activities within each chapter are grouped into four age ranges: preschoolers, kindergartners, first and second graders, and third graders and older. Please note, however, that most of the activities are appropriate for a wide range of ages.

Some things to remember:

☆ An activity marked with a "+" is also appropriate for an older age group.

☆ Many games can be played anywhere, anytime. Avoid a set "play time"—play is a great teacher because it interests children and doesn't seem like "work."

☆ Start slowly. Piling on too much, too quickly, can lead to frustration, a great enemy of developing concentration.

☆ Give your child lots of encouragement.

CHAPTER FOUR

Arts, Crafts, and Tactile Experiences

We begin the activities portion of this book with a chapter that focuses on things children can do with their hands. As we've already seen, concentration is not merely about focusing your mind on facts and figures. We've also seen how developmental experts readily acknowledge the importance of different sensory inputs both in the process of acquiring knowledge as well as in the context of different children's legitimate learning style differences.

Tray Weaving +

What you need: Styrofoam tray, construction paper cut into strips (about three-quarters of an inch wide), scissors

Here's something that not only helps younger children focus their attention on a task that's fun and productive, it also provides, at long last, a use for those otherwise useless styrofoam trays that sometimes come under meat, vegetables, and fruit.

To start, thoroughly wash the tray with detergent. You can let your child dry it. Next, put it on a cutting board and make parallel horizontal slits in the tray, about three-quarters of an inch or so apart. Your child's job is now to "weave" the strips of construction paper into the tray. It teaches the value of certain sorts of repetitive tasks, while producing a tangible result relatively quickly.

Remember:
Activities marked with a "+" are good for older children, too!

Make a Megaphone +

What you need: Empty plastic bottle, scissors, masking tape

This begins as a craft project—one which you will have to do for your child—and turns into an engaging way to play some simple listening games.

First, cut off the end of a two-liter plastic bottle, a couple of inches up from the bottom. Then tape the cut edge to be sure there are no sharp edges exposed. This is your megaphone. Show your child how your voice seems amplified when you speak through the narrow top. Let her try it, too.

One game you can play is a version of "Simon Says," in which your child follows your instruction only if the words ("Put your hands on your belly," etc.) are spoken through the megaphone. You can then switch and have her follow only those instructions spoken *not* through the megaphone. This can be made more challenging if your child keeps her eyes closed as you speak.

Another thing you can do is have your child wait in her bedroom while you go outside the room so she can hear you but not see you. You're going to count slowly to ten but use the megaphone for only one of the numbers. Tell her this is what you're going to do and when you're done you want her to bring you something from her room that relates to the number that you said through the megaphone. So if you used the megaphone for the number four, she can bring you four books or four shirts or four different things or even a picture of the number four in a book.

Secret Handshake +

It's fun, informative, and developmentally useful to apply concentration skills to more than writing, drawing, talking, and listening. Here's a little activity that allows your child to concentrate on body movements.

The goal is to invent a secret handshake, or a series of secret handshakes. You don't need a reason with children when it comes to secret handshakes; the idea is inherently appealing. (Although it doesn't hurt to offer a specific use—you might invent the "I've finished my homework" secret handshake, or the "I didn't watch any TV today" secret handshake.) Be creative in the process of creation—there are lots of movement options here. You might begin with the standard pump, and move quickly into left hand motions, hand claps, elbow bumps, finger fiddlings, and so forth.

> Here's a little activity that allows your child to concentrate on body movements.

Aim for a complex handshake, but build it step by step. You might take turns, and use the opportunity to "test" your child's concentration after each new stage is invented. Push him to see how involved a handshake he can remember.

Seeing with Your Fingers +

What you need: Cardboard box, glue, scissors, felt square the size of the box top, small objects from around the house

This "feel box" activity is a classic for a reason. Young children in particular love the excitement of reaching into a mysterious box and trying to "see" without their eyes. As a parent, you might like knowing that this sort of cross-sensory concentration is especially valuable in the development of overall concentration skills.

First, cut a circle in the top of the cardboard box, big enough for children to put a hand through. Draw the same size circle onto the felt square, then draw an X that divides the circle into quarters. Cut the slits that form the X but *not* the circle. Then glue the felt piece over the top of the box so that the circles line up.

Now place a small object inside the box. Let your child reach in and feel it carefully, then see if she can identify what's in her hand. Once she guesses, she can pull the object out and see if she knew what it was.

Another activity you can try involves placing a number of differently textured and/or shaped objects in the box and asking your child to find something smooth, something circular, and so forth.

Salty Designs +

What you need: Salt, roasting pan

This simple but intriguing activity helps encourage fine motor skills at an early age (see sidebar on page 31 for why this can be so important).

Pour a layer of salt in a roasting pan and have your child use it as a drawing board, using his finger. You can encourage him to make letters, draw pictures, even play tic-tac-toe. If he's just learning letters, you can draw the shapes first in the salt, then have him make his own next to yours.

Cereal Writing +

Who said excessively sweet breakfast cereals weren't good for something? In the case of Alpha-Bits®, here's a product with an unexpected benefit in the concentration building department.

Pour a half-cup or so of this letter-shaped cereal into a bowl in front of your child. Be sure her hands are clean. Put a napkin or paper towel down next to the bowl and have your child go to work in a variety of ways:

☆ have her sort the letters by type

☆ have her look for the letters A through Z, in order

☆ have her spell simple words

Or make up your own challenge. At the end, put the letters back in the bowl and, if the time is okay for a dessert or a sweet snack, pour some milk in and let her go at them the "normal" way.

ARTS, CRAFTS, AND TACTILE EXPERIENCES FOR KINDERGARTNERS

Squirt-Words +

This activity requires a warm day, some sort of squirting device, and an empty outdoor wall (one side or another of your house might do). Have your child take the squirter and try to write letters on the wall, or even such simple shapes as squares and triangles. This may take some practice to get the feel for controlling the water the right way.

Guesstimating +

Spatial concentration is put to the test in these related activities. First is a good bath-time activity, involving a standard (plastic) two-cup measure and a variety of other sized containers. Have your child choose one of the containers and study it for a moment. How much water does he think it will take to fill the container up? Show him the cup measure and tell him you'd like him to fill it up with the amount of water he thinks the other container needs to be filled. With older children, you can make reference to the specific measurements on the side of the measuring cup. A younger child may merely need to be shown the lines on the cup.

Have him fill the measuring cup with his "guesstimate," and then have him pour the water he measured into the other container. If his first guess was not very close, you can have him guess how much more needs to be added to have the container filled.

With an older child, you can also play this game backwards—have him fill the odd-shaped container first, then guess how much water, in either ounces or cups, is now in the container. He can check his guess by pouring the water from the container into the measuring cup.

You can play Guesstimate on dry land as well, in a whole other medium. All you need is a basket or bin full of pennies. Have your child grab two handfuls of the coins and, before putting them on a table, guess how many he grabbed. Write down his guess, then have him count the pennies he took.

MORE ARTS, CRAFTS, AND TACTILE EXPERIENCES FOR KINDERGARTNERS

(see Preschooler section)

- ✸ Tray Weaving
- ✸ Make a Megaphone
- ✸ Secret Handshake
- ✸ Seeing with Your Fingers
- ✸ Salty Designs
- ✸ Cereal Writing

Graph Paper Patterns +

What you need: Graph paper, crayons or colored pencils

Designing patterns offers your child a wonderful chance to mix creativity with focused attention to detail. Have your child take a sheet of graph paper and sketch some ideas for patterns that might make a nice repeat design on a full sheet. Here are a few examples:

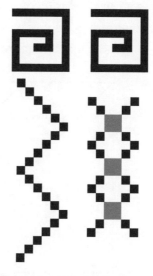

Be sure to have your child work with both shape and color. Once she has come upon a design which she likes, give her a new sheet and have her create the design in a repeating pattern around the entire page. As always, even though we have very definite goals in mind here, try to keep this from seeming like an assignment. You know best how to get your child interested. For instance, if your child likes to do what you do, you might try making some patterns yourself while your child is in the same room, ask for "help," and then watch her take off.

Tangram +

What you need: Cardboard or posterboard, pencil, scissors, blank paper

This classic puzzle from China is fun to make, and to reconstruct. Like most puzzles, it gives practice in recognizing spatial relationships and solving problems. But since the child helps make the puzzle in the first place, he also builds spatial memory *and* the habit of focusing in advance on information that will be useful later—the same habit that makes some people effective readers of recipes, economic analyses, or whodunits!

The basic tangram is a square that has been divided precisely into five triangles, a smaller square, and a rhomboid, like this:

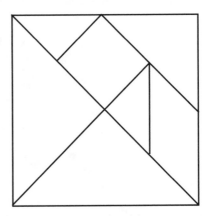

You can help your child create this figure with a pencil on a piece of cardboard or colored posterboard and then oversee the cutting of the pieces. Despite his having helped make the puzzle, once the pieces are scattered, it will take more than a little concentration to figure out how to reform the square. Once he does that, you can provide blank sheets of paper onto which he can invent and trace some of his own shapes, which he can later solve.

Color Blending

What you need: Good quality blank paper, oil pastels

For children used to drawing with either markers or crayons, oil pastels offer an amazing new artistic experience: color blending. An engaging little exercise requiring sustained attention can be made of the simple request to turn one color "into" another through blending.

Have your child create a band of color, perhaps one inch square, on the left side of the paper. On the right side of the paper, aligned with the first color, have her create a similarly sized band of

> **This is an engaging little exercise requiring sustained attention.**

another color, preferably an opposite-seeming color. Now instruct her to "change" the color on the left into the color on the right through steady blending.

You might have her practice a bit at first on another sheet of paper to help her get the hang of the basic idea of blending. The technique isn't difficult, and is repeatedly fixable—if she finds her color too dark, she can add more of the lighter color; if it gets too light, she can add more of the darker color, and on and on.

Make Your Own Mazes +

What you need: Blank paper, pencil

Once children become skilled at pencil and paper work, many grow fascinated with mazes, which are excellent concentration builders. Books of mazes are readily available in the children's section of many bookstores. You'll see the best results if the mazes you provide are just hard enough to challenge your child, but not so hard that he becomes frustrated and gives up. If your child gets "into" mazes, you can turn that interest into an even richer and more beneficial experience by prompting your child to make his own.

Showing your child how to construct his own mazes offers a new challenge, and a particularly enjoyable and multifaceted concentration exercise.

The easiest way to make a simple maze is to begin by drawing a square in the center of a page, with one opening, like this:

begin with

You might ask your child to draw a little picture in the center, to act as the "goal" of the maze. Next, have your child draw a series of three or four squares around the original square, each with one opening also; have the openings for each square occur in different places along the perimeter, so they don't line up, like this:

add squares around it, with openings

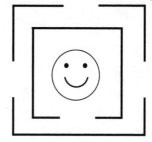

The maze begins at the opening in the outermost square. You could have your child draw an arrow there to mark it as the entrance. Then, have your child draw one perpendicular line blocking off the path within each "alley" between squares, like this:

and so on

Voilà! Your child has made a simple maze. By increasing the number of squares, as well as the number of openings and perpendicular blockages, he will make his maze more complex. Your child must pay attention as he does this, however, to be sure there is still a path that will take him from the beginning to the end.

The same method can be used to make a circular maze as well. As your child masters these simple mazes, he may decide to get into more free-form constructions. For younger children, it takes concentration enough merely to draw the maze with clarity and simple purpose. With older children, you can press them harder on keeping the maze workable as the complexity increases. As an extra incentive, you can offer to photocopy the final result, which can be distributed or sent around to various family members for completion.

MORE ARTS, CRAFTS, AND TACTILE EXPERIENCES FOR FIRST AND SECOND GRADERS

(see Preschooler section)
　✵ Secret Handshake

(see Kindergartner section)
　✵ Squirt-Words
　✵ Guesstimating

ARTS, CRAFTS, AND TACTILE EXPERIENCES FOR
THIRD GRADERS AND OLDER

Finger Calculation

From the Far East comes this really cool way of turning your child's fingers into a calculator that can add any numbers that equal 99 or less. It takes some careful, directed concentration at first, but the more your child practices, the faster she will be able to work her "calculator." As such, it's a great game for illustrating how concentration leads to new skills and abilities. Once your child masters this, next time she's frustrated over a new task remind her how confusing "finger calculation" was at first and how easy it became.

> This is a great game for illustrating how concentration leads to new skills and abilities.

The best way to teach your child how to do this is to learn it yourself first. Put your hands face down on a table, fingers spread. Each of the four fingers on your left hand represents 10, each of the four fingers on your right hand stands for 1. Your left thumb equals 50, while your right thumb equals 5. You register a number by folding the appropriate fingers under towards your palm. With your fingers all extended on both hands, your "calculator" actually reads 0; if both hands are folded up into fists, the number your hands are making is 99.

This will become more clear if we do a sample problem. We'll start with a simple one: 13 + 21. To start, fold in the index finger of your left hand (that's 10) plus your index, middle, and ring fingers on your right (that's 3). Your hands now show 13. To add 21, first convert it in your mind to groups of 10s and 1s (in this case, two 10s and one 1). Now "add" these numbers to

13 by folding in two more 10s on your left hand (the middle and ring fingers) and one more 1 on your right hand (the pinky).

If you did this right, you now have three fingers folded in on your left hand (equaling 30) and four fingers folded in on your right hand (equaling 4), which gives you the answer: 34.

Now we're ready for a slightly more complicated problem, which involves some exchanges between hands. Let's try 37 + 56. To begin, make 37. The 30 part is easy: fold in three fingers on your left hand. To make 7 on your right hand, use your thumb—which, remember, is 5—plus two fingers. How to add 56 to this? Easier than you think. Break down the number to 50 + 5 + 1. Add the 50 in a snap by folding in your left thumb. To add 5 now is the tricky part: What you do is first subtract 5 by unfolding your right thumb; then add 10 on the left hand by folding down one more finger. By subtracting 5 and adding 10 you've added 5. Fold down one more finger for the last 1, and you're left with your entire left hand folded in (90) plus three fingers folded in on your right hand (3), which is the answer: 93.

Super Secret Code

Older children often enjoy the challenge of working with secret codes. Here's an especially intriguing code mechanism that's easy to work with but impossible to figure out without the key.

To begin, make a box five squares across and five squares down, and fill it with the alphabet, like this. (Combine the letter J with the letter I to allow the letters to fit.)

A	B	C	D	E
F	G	H	I/J	K
L	M	N	O	P
Q	R	S	T	U
V	W	X	Y	Z

Believe it or not, this is your master code key. To make it work, you must first take the message you want to encode and convert it into groups of two letters. Say your message is: PANCAKES FOR DINNER. This, grouped by twos, turns first into: PA NC AK ES FO RD IN NE RZ. (You put a Z at the end if the message has an odd number of letters. There must always be groups of two.)

Now comes the trick. Take each letter pair and locate them on the grid. Use these two letters as opposite corners of an imagined square or rectangle; and then, with a pencil or in your mind, complete the shape. For example, for the letter pair PA, you would imagine a large rectangle that would have P in the bottom right and A in the upper left. Completing this rectangle you'd find E in the upper right and L in the lower left. Now, take the original two letters and swap them for the letters either above or below them in the rectangle. In this case, you'd end up with E for the P and L for the A. So your encoded letter pair is EL.

Think about this for a moment; it's not nearly as complicated as it looks. Once you've gotten the hang of it, you'll have to know about a few exceptions. First, take a look at the next pair in our example: NC. You'll notice that both letters are in the same column, so you can't use them to create a square or rectangle. In this case, you simply stay in the column and move down to get a new letter for each—that is, you move down to S for the N and down to H for the C. So the encoded letter pair is SH.

When the two letters appear in the same row, move to the right for each to get the new letter. For example, LO would become MP. If one of the letters is the last in its row or column, go back to the beginning or the top to get the encoded letter. Thus, for instance, PZ would become UE. The last exception occurs when both letters in the pair are the same. In this case, move down one—HH, for example, would become NN.

The fully encoded sample message will end up reading: EL SH FE UC LJ BT OH CP WU. To make this truly impenetrable, separate these randomly into different sized "words"—perhaps FE UCLJB TOH CPWU.

To decode, you apply the same rules—first grouping into pairs, then forming squares or rectangles when possible. When letters are in the same row or column, however, you must apply a reverse direction for decoding, moving to the left when the letters share a row, moving up when both letters are in the same column, and moving up if there are two of the same letter.

MORE ARTS, CRAFTS, AND TACTILE EXPERIENCES FOR THIRD GRADERS AND OLDER

(see Preschooler section)
  ✡ Secret Handshake

(see Kindergartner section)
  ✡ Guesstimating

(see First and Second Grader section)
  ✡ Graph Paper Patterns
  ✡ Tangram
  ✡ Make Your Own Mazes

CHAPTER FIVE

Talking and Listening Games

This chapter offers an involving selection of activities that focus on listening and speaking. Some of these are classic children's games, while others will probably be new to you. The intent with all of them is to direct your child's attention onto specific tasks, often involving perseverance, within an atmosphere of fun.

Skip Counting +

Once your child is old enough to count reliably to at least twenty, here's a quick game that promotes attention and can even help develop some basic math skills.

What you are going to do is count to twenty but leave numbers out along the way that your child has to provide. You might want to use some sort of pointing device, even just a pencil, to help her know when you're asking for a number from her. The first few times the two of you will proceed haltingly. Keep working at it; strive to count in a steady rhythm.

The easiest way to achieve this is to leave "blanks" at regular intervals. You might say, "One... two..." then point to your child for "Three," after which you say, "Four... five..." and point to the child for "Six," and so on. Once you work this to a steady rhythm, you can talk afterward about how you can "hear" multiples this way. (And see the activity "Musical Multiples" in the *Music, Sound, and Movement* chapter for a cool variation of this idea.)

But the real challenge of this game will be to leave blanks randomly and still see how steadily the two of you together can count. As your child improves, you can increase the pace of the counting.

Remember:
Activities marked with a "+" are good for older children, too!

Fill in the Blanks +

How closely does your child listen to something he's never heard before? Use this entertaining game to find out.

What you'll need is a big book of children's poems, whether Mother Goose or some other rhythmic verses. Find a poem with two or three verses that you know your child has never heard before. Tell him you are going to

> This game shows your child how quickly his mind can memorize things.

read him a new poem once. He should listen carefully, because you want to show him how quickly his mind can memorize things.

After you read it the first time, explain how you will now read it again but will leave out certain words. He should fill them in. For instance, say you read the poem "Bed in Summer," by Robert Louis Stevenson. The first time through, you'd read:

In winter I get up at night
And dress by yellow candlelight.
In summer, quite the other way,
I have to go to bed by day.

I have to go to bed and see
The birds still hopping on the tree,
Or hear the grown-up people's feet
Still going past me in the street.

And does it not seem hard to you,
When all the sky is clear and blue,
And I should like so much to play,
To have to go to bed by day?

Then, the second time through, you might read:

In winter, I get up at night
And dress by yellow _____.
In summer, quite the other way,
I have to go to bed by _____.

I have to go to _____ and see
The birds still hopping on the _____,
Or hear the grown-up _____ feet
Still going past me in the _____.

And does it not seem _____ to you
When all the _____ is clear and _____,
And I should like so much to _____,
To have to go to bed by _____?

As you can see, it's a good idea to help get your child started, to allow him to remember through the rhymes. But challenge him later in the poem with some words that he must also remember without the help of a rhyme.

Can You Hear Me? +

Some talking games involve comprehension-oriented concentration, like "Ghost," at the end of this chapter. This one, for younger children, develops simple but important listening-oriented concentration.

You need a relatively large room; outside works also. Begin with you and your child facing one another, a couple of feet apart. The gist of the game is that you will say a phrase, quietly but not whispering, and she has to repeat it. A good way to keep your mind focused on phrases is to use alliterative phrases, beginning with A. So you might start with "absent-minded aardvarks!" or something like that. Once your child repeats the phrase, each of you backs up a long step. Then say another phrase ("beautiful beavers!")—again, quietly but not whispering. Your child should repeat it full strength. Both of you back up another step. Say another phrase, and have your child repeat it.

The aim of the game is to see how far apart you can get before your child misses the phrase. Once your child can no longer hear and repeat your phrase, you can take a tape measure and record how far apart you got. When you play it again you can see if you can get farther.

Opposite Day +

To focus children on a longer-term concentration project, you might try announcing that today is going to be "Opposite Day." On Opposite Day, everyone is to use words meaning the opposite of what they really mean. "Time to go to sleep!" you might announce to them as you rouse them in the morning (if your children need rousing, that is). You can tell them, "Take your time!" when you need them to hurry.

And so forth.

By Heart +

Back in the olden days (that is, thirty years ago or more), students in school from an early age were taught to memorize all sorts of things, from lengthy poems to the letters of the Greek alphabet to the preamble to the Constitution of the United States. This kind of rote approach to education has long since fallen into disfavor for many reasons. But as it turns out, there is something to be said for a bit of good old-fashioned memorization every now and then, especially when it comes to improving concentration.

That said, we can certainly do without reciting dry strings of words or facts. Traditional poems, on the other hand, are just about ready-made for memorization, thanks to their rhythms

> An occasional bit of good old-fashioned memorization helps improve concentration.

and rhymes. Younger children can start with simple Mother Goose rhymes. You can point out how they already know many such rhymes by heart. For this memorization exercise, have your child pick from a book a Mother Goose poem that he doesn't already know. (All Mother Goose books have many less familiar rhymes in addition to the most widely known ones.) If he can read already, write it out neatly for him and keep it handy for his perusal. If he doesn't read yet, go over the poem daily line by line. It shouldn't take much effort for a short poem. Keep the encouragement strong and move him next onto a slightly longer poem, and then a longer one. Once he knows four or five, you can suggest he put on a "poetry show" for the whole family; you might even videotape it so he can see himself afterward.

Older children might sink their memorization teeth into an entertaining poem such as "Casey at the Bat" by Ernest

Lawrence Thayer ("The outlook wasn't brilliant for the Mudville nine that day...") or "Paul Revere's Ride" by Henry Wadsworth Longfellow ("Listen, my children, and you shall hear...").

MORE TALKING AND LISTENING GAMES FOR KINDERGARTNERS

(see Preschooler section)
   ☆ Skip Counting

Tongue Twisters +

Once your child is speaking clearly—usually by the first grade if not before—tongue twisters offer a fun opportunity to put concentration skills to a tangible test. Our list here is just a sample; feel free to invent your own. But understand that tongue twisters are most challenging when the letter sounds shift in ways that force your mouth to move in awkward ways. Often you'll see phrases or sentences labeled tongue twisters that are merely extended alliterations, and not actually the least bit difficult to say. The list here, on the other hand, is comprised of serious tongue twisters. The shorter phrases at the beginning of the list are especially tricky when attempted three times, as quickly as possible.

- Swiss wristwatch
- Knapsack straps
- Greek grapes
- Mixed biscuits
- Flash message
- Peggy Babcock (This one is much harder than it looks!)
- Red lorry, yellow lorry
- Mrs. Smith's Fish Sauce Shop
- Tim, the thin twin tinsmith
- Friendly Frank flips fine flapjacks
- The sixth sick sheik's sixth sheep's sick
- Old oily Ollie oils old oily autos

Backwards Bee +

Children who pride themselves on their spelling ability will find unexpected fun in the challenge of having to spell words backward. Start your child out with some simple words to give her a chance to get the hang of it. Younger children will want to stick with three- and four-letter words for the entire "Bee"; even so, you should try to move past standard fare such as "dog" and "cat" and into some more interesting short words such as "owl," "why," and "quiz." Older children may still need reasonably short words to start with (after all, can *you* spell hippopotamus backwards, without a pen and paper handy?)

> This—and many other games—can be offered informally, even in the car.

As with many of the activities in this book, the Backwards Bee can be offered informally, perhaps as you're driving in the car or waiting in line somewhere, or can be organized in a more "official" way. The informal approach can be fun and useful, but many children may also be pleasantly excited if the Backwards Bee is handled like a special event. You might explain it in advance and set it up to be held at a specific time later that day—you can even make a small sign advertising this fact. During the Bee itself, you can keep score, and save the scores for comparison next time. For many children, this sort of "official" Bee is more likely to hold their interest—and, therefore, keep their concentration focused—than a more casual "hey, let's spell some words backward" approach.

Fast Talking +

A whole different sort of concentration is required when your child is not attempting to memorize something but merely to say it as quickly as possible. This game gets silly quickly, but there's something compelling about it for kids, especially when there's a stopwatch and scoring involved.

Simply pick out a short, familiar poem for your child to try to say as quickly as he possibly can. With younger children, something very familiar, such as "Little Miss Muffet," works best. Even older children are likely to work best with Mother Goose rhymes for this game, since you want the words to be already embedded in their heads; the idea is for them not to trip over words they're reading for the first time.

You can make a chart and time your child on a variety of poems. Go back to it every now and then, and see if he can beat any of his old times.

I You Yes No +

An intriguing dialogue game, "I You Yes No" tells you, in the title, the words that one player must not say, while the other player tries to trick her into saying one of them.

One player plays the role of a shopkeeper, the other plays the role of the customer coming into the store. The shopkeeper asks the customer questions, which she must answer without saying any one of those four words. For instance, the shopkeeper might say, "Good morning, madam! How are you today?" The customer could say, "Fine, thanks," but not "I'm fine." The shopkeeper might say, "Our tomatoes are especially fresh today. Would you like some?" To which the customer might say, "Perhaps later," but not "No, thanks," or "I don't think so." And so forth. The game lasts as long as the shopkeeper can keep thinking of questions and the customer can answer them.

To keep the customer honest, she should not be allowed to use the same answer twice in a row (to avoid having the player latch onto the answer "Maybe," for instance).

If you think it's easy, give it a try.

MORE TALKING AND LISTENING GAMES FOR FIRST AND SECOND GRADERS

(see Kindergartner section)
- ✵ Fill in the Blanks
- ✵ Can You Hear Me?
- ✵ Opposite Day
- ✵ By Heart

Ghost

This is an oldie but goodie that goes under many different names. This version is called "Ghost" for no readily apparent reason; in any case, the word *ghost* is used to keep track of how the players are doing—each time you lose a round, you get a letter from the word; once you get G-H-O-S-T, you're out.

Ghost is a spelling game and therefore best with older children, although spelling-oriented second-graders are likely to enjoy it as well. You need at least two players—three or four are even better. The first player names a letter to start the round. The second player must then call out a letter that can follow the first letter in a legitimate English word, but does not itself *complete* a word. The next player does the same thing—names a letter that can follow the other two in a real word but does not now form a word. Play continues until someone is stuck—he cannot think of a letter to add to the string of letters which can be part of a longer word but does not itself complete a word. If at any point someone uses a letter that creates a combination of letters which another player doesn't think will lead to a word, he can be challenged.

For example, say the first player said the letter S. The second player might say the letter A (if he said the letter O here, he'd be out, for completing the word "so"). The next player could then say N—but not T or Y or G. The player who follows the N might say I if there are three or more players—he might be hoping to push the word "sanity" or "sanitation" (if there were only two players, these words would end on him, which he wouldn't want).

You should have a dictionary handy for challenges. You can play that anyone can challenge anyone else at any point, or, to add to the difficulty, you can play that anyone who challenges someone incorrectly gets a letter himself. This reduces the number of frivolous challenges.

Whoever ultimately gets stuck at the end of the round gets the letter G and a new round is started. The game is over when all players but one receive the letters G-H-O-S-T.

MORE TALKING AND LISTENING GAMES FOR THIRD GRADERS AND OLDER

(see Kindergartner section)
　　✻ By Heart

(see First and Second Grader section)
　　✻ Tongue Twisters
　　✻ Backwards Bee
　　✻ Fast Talking
　　✻ I You Yes No

CHAPTER SIX

Music, Sound, and Movement

Sounds, rhythms, and movements of all kinds are not only fun for children—they are also often linked to how children learn and remember. The activities in this section use music, sound, and general moving around in a variety of ways, both expected and unexpected.

MUSIC, SOUND, AND MOVEMENT FOR
PRESCHOOLERS

What Sound Do You Hear? +

Like it or not, ours is a world full of noises. This is a simple activity you can do with your young child, ideally on a walk up and down your street. Ask "What sound do you hear?" and push your child beyond saying, "Nothing" or "I don't know." There are almost always birds or cars and trucks or airplanes or insects or people's voices in the background. Directing your child to pay attention to background sounds he might not otherwise hear is a subtle but sure way to improve concentration skills.

Remember:
Activities marked with a "+" are good for older children, too!

What Is It? +

This is another sound identification game, but one in which you control the sounds your child will try to name. You should gather a variety of things that can make distinguishable noises— a bell, a pair of scissors (you can make a cutting sound), a few coins (they can be jingled together), a paperback book (you can riffle the pages), a dry leaf (crumble it), and so forth. These things should be hidden in a box or bag out of view.

Set up a place where you can take each item out, one by one, and make the noise so that your child can hear it but can't see it. Have her guess what's making the sound. If she doesn't get it after hearing it a few times, put the item aside but don't show it to her yet—come back to it later after going through all the sounds once.

The best place to set this game up is behind a puppet theater of some kind if you happen to have one. Or you can block your child's vision with an easel or a large chair. (In a pinch, sitting around a corner from one another in your house may work for some, but other children may feel less engaged that way.)

Bombs Away +

Whenever you feel a need for a well-deserved break from talking or writing or listening or remembering games, here's one that promotes kinesthetic concentration.

You'll need a decent-sized room, three successively larger buckets or bins, and three or more wooden clothespins (or some other objects of similar size and weight). The small bucket should be reasonably small but still large enough to fit the clothespin. None of them should be too shallow.

Place the buckets in a row on the floor, each about five or six inches from one another. Put the smallest one on the left, the largest one in the middle, and the medium-sized one on the right. Start your child seven or eight feet away (or more, if you have room) from the medium-sized bin; if he were to run straight at them, they should be parallel with his path and just off to his right (or left, if he's left-handed).

Yes, he *is* going to run at them. But first hand him a clothespin. His job, you can explain, is to run quickly past the buckets and try to drop the clothespin into one of them. The small bucket is worth twenty-five points, the large one five points, the medium-sized one ten points. Give him three turns and add up his score. Let him do as many rounds as he has energy for, and see how his score improves.

Now Ear This +

We all went to the school nurse's office as children and had the yearly hearing test. It was fun, wasn't it?: Put the headphones on, listen carefully, raise your right hand if you hear the sound in your right ear, your left hand if you hear the sound in your left. Well, here's a way you can re-create this inherently engaging concentration test with your child at home.

All you need is an effective blindfold. Sit your child down in a chair you can approach comfortably from the back. Tie the blindfold and be sure she cannot see even a little out the bottom or sides. From behind now, use your fingers to make quiet sounds near one or another of her ears. Have her raise the hand on the side she hears the sound. Vary the volume of the sounds, from loud snaps to the quiet rubbing of two fingers.

> Here's an inherently engaging concentration test.

For a fun variation with a younger child, you can whisper in one ear a word that has an opposite, and have your child say the word's opposite as she raises her hand.

Invent-a-Dance +

Young children have an innate joy for dancing that should be encouraged as deeply as possible. Many experts, furthermore, believe that applying concentration skills to movement-oriented activities can be another effective way of helping your child's overall attention span. Thus the impetus for "Invent-a-Dance."

Begin with some of your child's favorite music. Tell him you would like him to create a dance designed exclusively for this music. Start by just listening—encourage him to feel the music deep within his body. When he feels like moving, have him start slowly, concentrating on his movements. You would like him not only to create a new dance but also to be able to teach it to you step by step. This may involve having him focus some of his energy into smaller or more conscious bursts.

When the song you're listening to is over, stop it and play it again. Have your child re-create the dance; he can fine-tune some of the movements, or simply do it all over again. Tell him that after the song is done the second time, he should be able to start teaching you the dance as well. When the song is over the second time, see if he is ready to show you some of the moves, without the music. Then turn the music on again and let him instruct you step by step.

Do your best to keep him focused, but don't spoil the spontaneity and the joy of the movement. And don't forget to have fun yourself!

Letter Hop +

A little sidewalk chalk and an empty driveway go a long way in this game, which tests your child's alphabet knowledge in a kinesthetic setting.

What you are going to do is write the alphabet, scrambled, on the driveway. Do this with your child's assistance: Have her call out the first letter (namely, A) and show you where on the driveway she wants you to write it. Then have her say "B" and run to the spot where the B should go. Gently guide her to keep the letters in one relatively defined space but also reasonably well mixed up. If your child is especially good at letter recognition, you can vary them by writing them at all different angles, so some of them she'll have to recognize on their sides or upside down.

When you get to Z, bring your child back off the letter area and ask her to find the letter A and run to it. Tell her you are going to call out a letter she is going to find, as well as a method to get there. So you might say "Jump to B"; when she gets there, you might then say "Hop to C," and so forth. You can increase the challenge by going out of order (which will force a greater level of concentration), and even calling two or three letters at once, including different instructions for getting from one to the next.

Higher or Lower? +

You need neither musical ability nor any formal musical instruments in the house to take your child through this very simple exercise in sound awareness and concentration.

All you need is some sort of instrument that can play a certain variety of notes—perhaps a toy keyboard, a xylophone, a recorder, or a harmonica. Tell your child you are going to play two different notes. You would like him to listen and then tell you which note was higher and which note was lower. With younger children, you may have to review the overall concept of high and low sounds. With older children, you can keep them challenged by playing notes that are very close together.

Beat It! +

Most memory games involve visual stimuli. Here's a fun alternative that tests your child's ability to concentrate on and remember sound.

The sound in question is one of a younger child's all-time favorites: drumbeats. Even better, these are drumbeats produced by banging your hands or fingers on a table. To begin, sit down with your child at a table that can withstand a

> Here's a fun activity that tests your child's ability to concentrate on and remember sound.

little good-natured banging. Bang out a simple beat, and ask your child to repeat it. Increase the complexity to suit her ability.

**MUSIC, SOUND, AND MOVEMENT FOR
KINDERGARTNERS**

Countdown +

This activity can be done with one of your child's favorite music tapes, or you can provide the singing yourself. The idea is for your child to count the number of times a certain word appears in the song. With younger children, it's easiest to sing a simple song yourself—perhaps "Mary Had a Little Lamb" (have your child count the number of times he hears the word "lamb").

**MORE MUSIC, SOUND, AND MOVEMENT FOR
KINDERGARTNERS**

(see Preschooler section)
   ✻ What Sound Do You Hear?
   ✻ What Is It?
   ✻ Bombs Away
   ✻ Now Ear This
   ✻ Invent-a-Dance
   ✻ Letter Hop
   ✻ Higher or Lower?
   ✻ Beat It!

Name That Tune +

This old game-show concept is just the thing to sharpen concentration skills. This will work best if you set up a little in advance. With a tape player, take a bunch of music tapes that are familiar to your child (ten or twelve would be good, if you have the patience) and set them each up at the beginning of a song. Then call your child over and explain the premise—namely, that you are going to play the very beginning of a song that she knows, just a short snippet. She should listen very carefully and then see if she can tell you what song it is.

> This old game-show concept is just the thing to sharpen concentration skills.

You will have to adjust the length of the snippets you play to the age and ability of your child. At the beginning she may need five seconds or more. As she gets the hang of it, you may find she can name a song after hearing only one second, or even less! If you have a double-deck tape player, you may find that it is actually easier to make a game tape with several song bits on it than to cue up ten different tapes and shuffle them in and out of the tape player.

If your child is old enough and has interest in popular music on the radio, this can be a fun game to play in the car, also. Tune the radio to her favorite station, but keep the volume down. Then, turn the sound up for just a quick blast of music. See if she can name the song you tuned into.

MORE MUSIC, SOUND, AND MOVEMENT FOR FIRST AND SECOND GRADERS

(see Preschooler section)
- ✵ Bombs Away
- ✵ Now Ear This
- ✵ Invent-a-Dance
- ✵ Higher or Lower?
- ✵ Beat It!

(see Kindergartner section)
- ✵ Countdown

MUSIC, SOUND, AND MOVEMENT FOR THIRD GRADERS AND OLDER

Musical Multiples

This counting exercise uses rhythm to reinforce concentration and multiplication at the same time. Having two, three, or even four children participate is ideal, but you can do it with just one child, also.

You need to have a simple percussion instrument or wind instrument for each child, plus something that can act as a basic drum for yourself. Each child should be assigned a number between two and six. (If you're working with just one child, have him take two, three, or four.) You will take the number one.

Begin counting slowly from one to sixty (you might be able to do this with second graders also, but in that case you might want to go only to thirty). What each person does is bang on or blow into his instrument when the count arrives at a number that is a multiple of his assigned number. This means, to begin with, that you bang on your drum with each number, because each number is a multiple of one.

If you play with just one child, your child will hear only his own multiples, which is an interesting enough exercise, especially for younger children. (If you try this with a second grader, for instance, you might want to have only the one child involved, so as not to confuse him.) If you play with three or four children, however, an extra wonderful thing happens as the count proceeds: Those numbers (such as twelve and twenty-four) that have three or more multiples sound loudest; prime numbers, on the other hand, are distinguished by just your drumbeat. This complex but engaging concentration activity literally allows the children to "hear" math.

MORE MUSIC, SOUND, AND MOVEMENT FOR
THIRD GRADERS AND OLDER

(see First and Second Grader section)
  ☆ Name That Tune

CHAPTER SEVEN

Perception and Performance

The activities and games in this chapter offer many different takes on visually oriented concentration skills, independent of reading or listening. In this camp you'll find a variety of spins on the classic game of "Concentration" (and how could we leave out the original?), as well as some new ways of turning concentration improvement into fun.

Letter Hunt +

Before your child knows how to read, you can focus his concentration on letter recognition with this simple activity.

Pull out a book of his, and instead of reading it to him, have him hunt for letters. You can proceed in alphabetical order if you'd like, or choose letters randomly—have him hunt for an E, then an R, then a B, and so on.

It's fun for him to use a magazine for this game as well. Children like to look at Mommy's or Daddy's magazines; this gives them a fun job to do as they browse.

Remember:
Activities marked with a "+" are good for older children, too!

Photographic Memory +

This memory exercise challenges younger children to pay close attention to familiar pictures; for older children, the challenge becomes how thoroughly they can absorb unfamiliar visual input.

The basic gist is the same for each: You show your child a picture for a limited amount of time, and then have her answer questions about it without being able to look at it. With a younger child, choose an interesting, reasonably involved picture from one of her storybooks. Start with such simple questions as "What color was the dog?" "Were there any people in the picture?" "Was the picture inside or outside?" You can increase the challenge by asking about numbers ("How many flowers were there?") or facial specifics ("Did anyone have glasses?") And, obviously, you can make it harder by allowing a shorter time to study the picture.

Working with an older child, you might want to choose a picture from one of your own magazines (with appropriate content, of course!). When you ask your questions, you can even misdirect. "What was the woman in the hat doing?" you might ask—knowing that there was no woman with a hat.

Back Writing +

When your child has been recognizing letters reliably for a year or so, he is ready to put that skill to a test that combines concentration efforts in an intriguing, cross-sensory way.

> Test your child's concentration in an intriguing, cross-sensory way.

The game is simple: Have your child stand with his back to you, while you draw a capital letter with your finger on his back. Draw it reasonably large, and slowly. See if he can guess what letter it is.

With older children the game can be expanded to involve short words or names.

Don't Forget! +

Observational concentration is tested tantalizingly in this game, which requires a tray and an assortment of household objects. Gather the items without your child watching, scatter them on the tray (perhaps ten for younger children, twenty or more for older children), and then cover the tray. Bring the tray to your child, and give her one minute to study it. Then remove the tray from the room.

Now your child must attempt to list everything that was on the tray. If she is not old enough to write, have her list them out loud, and you can write them down.

This game will greatly reward your child with repeated efforts. A worthwhile variation of this game can be played by having your child study the tray as before, removing the tray from your child's sight as before, but then bringing it back minus one of the original items. See how quickly your child can figure out what's missing.

Egg Carton Match +

This game requires two empty egg cartons and can be played in a simpler or more complex way, depending on the age of the child.

For younger children, take one of the egg cartons and place one small household object in each of six egg holders. These should be objects the child can recognize, and he should also know where to find similar items in your house. Perhaps you'll want to put a penny in one egg holder, a Cheerio® in another, a rubber band in another, and so forth. Show your child the items you've placed in your egg carton, and then close the carton. Your child must now go and find the same objects and place them in his own egg carton.

To increase the challenge with age, you can require your child to find the same objects and put them in the same positions in his egg carton. You can also increase the number of objects to eight or even ten; you can decrease the viewing time as well. And finally, for the ultimate challenge, you can introduce a deadline and have your child attempt to do it all in a certain amount of time.

Concentration Classic +

What book with activities aimed at improving concentration could fail to include Concentration? Actually, as you'll see, we have a few different types of Concentration. Let's start with the classic, playing-card version.

This one is fun for younger children to set up and play because first of all it involves making a reasonably big-looking mess. Take a deck of fifty-two playing cards and spread them out face down on the floor. They don't have to be in any

> In this book, we have several different versions of "Concentration."

particular pattern at all. (To make a more manageable game for younger children, you can preselect a smaller number of cards, perhaps twenty-four, as long as they are all pairs.)

Children also seem to have an inherent joy in memory matching games, which is what this is. Take turns turning over two cards. You are looking for matches—numerical matches in the case of the ace through ten cards, letter matches in the case of the picture cards. If the cards your child turns over do not match, she turns them back over in place and it's your turn. Soon enough you'll be turning over cards that match something someone has already turned over. Can you remember where it was?

Object Concentration +

This Concentration requires a bit of set-up the first time, but after that it's easy. To begin with, you'll need some large plastic drinking cups. Turn them upside down and number them with an indelible marker from one to twenty-four or one to thirty, depending on how big you want the game. Next, gather a series of paired household items—twelve pairs if you use twenty-four cups, fifteen pairs if you use thirty cups. These objects have to be small enough to be concealed entirely beneath the cups. These can be things like two batteries, two nails, two pen caps, etc.

Pebble Concentration +

This Native American game offers us a truly intriguing variation on the Concentration theme. Two players, each holding the same number of pebbles, sit back to back on the ground. One player uses his pebbles to create a pattern of any kind. When he's done, the second player turns to look at the design for one minute. Then, he turns around and attempts to duplicate the pattern with his own pebbles. If he gets it, then it's his turn to create the design. If not, the first player goes again.

You can tailor the number of pebbles to the age of the child. Roughly a handful is a good gauge—which may mean eight or ten for younger players, fifteen or more for older ones.

MORE PERCEPTION AND PERFORMANCE FOR KINDERGARTNERS

(see Preschooler section)
☆ Letter Hunt

**PERCEPTION AND PERFORMANCE FOR
FIRST AND SECOND GRADERS**

Speed Concentration +

Here's an unusual variation on the Concentration theme in which the cards start face up. Spread them on the floor as in the classic set-up; you can use the whole deck, or just part of it. You'll also need a stopwatch or a watch with a second hand.

Have your child look the cards over for a minute or so. The object is for her to gather the cards as quickly as possible as you call the names out. Begin by saying, "On your mark... get set... King of Diamonds!" (or whatever card you choose first). Keep your own eye carefully on the cards as well, so you are always ready with the name of the next card for her to find.

See how long it takes for her to gather the whole deck. You can record the time and compare it as you play the game again down the road.

What Do You ABC? +

If you can find a few large, involved photographs from a magazine, you can use them to play a challenging, alphabet-oriented concentration game.

All players (you can play with two or more) begin by listing the letters of the alphabet down the left side of the paper. The goal is to find something in the photo that begins with each letter. Now, obviously, there may not be something for all twenty-six letters, but give it your best shot in either two or three minutes. Do not write more than one thing per letter; if you see two or more things, choose the one you think the other players might not write down. The players should be sitting so that they can all see the photograph but not each other's lists.

When time is up, compare lists. Anything on more than one player's list is crossed out. Score one point for anything you have that no other player listed. You can play as many rounds as you have photographs. Or, you can split the alphabet into A–M and N–Z, and use each photograph twice.

Seconds Count +

How closely can your child estimate passing time? Trying to count seconds as they pass offers your child an unusual opportunity to attempt a remarkable feat of concentration.

All you need is a watch with a second hand. Tell your child you would like him, by counting the seconds in his head, to tell you when thirty seconds have passed. Give him an "On your mark, get set, go!" and see how he does.

Children vary widely on this exercise. Many are fascinated by the effort. If your child misses by a lot, have him look at the second hand himself for thirty seconds, and then try again. If he does very well, try him at sixty seconds.

Word Hunt +

How many new, smaller words can your child form by using the letters contained in one larger word? That's the basic gist of this classic game.

Write a word on a blank piece of paper and have your child use the letters to form as many other words as she can. Choose a familiar word with a nice mix of letters; it can be relatively short, like "tower," or somewhat longer, like "decorate." (Tip: It's good to have at least one "e" in the word.)

Many daily newspapers, by the way, have this game on the same page as the comics; older children should be able to use this on the spot.

Instructions +

It's one thing to apply concentration skills to a game situation. Can your child concentrate on everyday tasks? Here's how to make of game of this.

Choose a very simple act that your child does easily and often—perhaps brushing his teeth, or opening a door, or reading a book. Tell him you would like him to create foolproof instructions for this act—instructions which break down the action to every last step. For brushing his teeth, for instance, he can't just say "Put toothpaste on toothbrush." He'd have to say: "1) Pick up toothpaste tube. 2) Unscrew cap. 3) Put cap next to sink. 4) Pick up toothbrush. 5) Squeeze small amount of toothpaste on toothbrush. 6) Put toothpaste down."

> You can even make a game of concentrating on everyday tasks.

Oops!—he forgot to screw the cap back on. That's very important, as we know.

Younger children may need help writing down their instructions. Older children can be encouraged to design theirs to look like an actual set of instructions that might come with a new appliance.

Morse Code +

Somewhere between first and third grade, many children grow fascinated with the idea of secret codes. Having them study and learn Morse code is a wonderful exercise in concentration development not only because of the memorization required but for the discernment skills necessary to "read" incoming messages.

First, here's the basic code:

A	. _	S	. . .
B	_ . . .	T	_
C	_ . _ .	U	. . _
D	_ . .	V	. . . _
E	.	W	. _ _
F	. . _ .	X	_ . . _
G	_ _ .	Y	_ . _ _
H	. . . .	Z	_ _ . .
I	. .	1	. _ _ _ _
J	. _ _ _	2	. . _ _ _
K	_ . _	3	. . . _
L	. _ . .	4	. . . . _
M	_ _	5	. . . . .
N	_ .	6	_ . . . .
O	_ _ _	7	_ _ . . .
P	. _ _ .	8	_ _ _ . .
Q	_ _ . _	9	_ _ _ _ .
R	. _ .	0	_ _ _ _ _

Be sure to tell your child about what Morse code was originally used for and why. It seems almost astonishingly primitive to a child of the 1990s to think that the only way people used to be able to communicate over long distances was through this mysterious combination of "dots" and "dashes."

A good way for a child to begin to test her knowledge of Morse code is through flash cards. Once she's pretty confident in her knowledge, it's time to turn reading dots and dashes into listening for short and long taps. Clicking the backs of two spoons together is one good way to create Morse code "signals." You could also tap on the wall. Or you can opt for a visual signal by using a flashlight.

On the Other Hand... +

Everyone has two hands, but we of course do many important tasks with just one of them. By "forcing" your child to attempt to use his weaker hand for some major jobs, you will require an especially focused and physically oriented concentration.

Begin by having your child do an everyday task like eating cereal or brushing his teeth with the "wrong" hand. These sorts of things will seem awkward; even a seemingly simple, automatic thing like scrubbing your teeth with toothpaste becomes an activity demanding particular attention when performed with a normally unused hand.

The real fun begins when you see how your child can write without using his dominant hand. Have him warm up by writing each letter of the alphabet. Then see how he does on his name and address. Not only is this difficult, but it will also probably seem very tiring to your child, both mentally and physically. As such, you can be sure his concentration is getting a good workout.

MORE PERCEPTION AND PERFORMANCE FOR FIRST AND SECOND GRADERS

(see Kindergartner section)

- Photographic Memory
- Back Writing
- Don't Forget!
- Egg Carton Match
- Concentration Classic
- Object Concentration
- Pebble Concentration

Lip Reading

Do you think you and your child can communicate if she can speak normally but you can only move your lips? Take five minutes of your day to see. Help her out by speaking slowly and with a certain amount of exaggerated mouth movements. Notice which words or sounds are easiest for her to understand, and use more of those.

Clearly this focuses your child's concentration in a very particular way; the built-in reward is comprehension. If she stays with it, and you do this repeatedly, she will acquire an intriguing new skill.

MORE PERCEPTION AND PERFORMANCE FOR THIRD GRADERS AND OLDER

(see Kindergartner section)
- ✺ Photographic Memory
- ✺ Back Writing
- ✺ Don't Forget!
- ✺ Egg Carton Match
- ✺ Pebble Concentration

(see First and Second Grader section)
- ✺ Speed Concentration
- ✺ What Do You ABC?
- ✺ Seconds Count
- ✺ Word Hunt
- ✺ Instructions
- ✺ Morse Code
- ✺ On the Other Hand...

PART THREE

Concentration: Building Block for Success and Happiness

CHAPTER EIGHT

Concentration, Television, and Video Games

In his book *Touchpoints*, a guide to emotional and behavioral development, well-known pediatrician T. Berry Brazelton asserts that, other than a child's family, there is no force today that influences behavior as powerfully as television. For every social advocate who suggests that television and video games are not good for children, there seems to be a counterpart to suggest that if it is carefully monitored and the amount of exposure limited, television has some distinct advantages. About the only clear thing that emerges from this ongoing debate is the idea that, for better or worse, TV is unlikely to go away anytime soon.

In this book, we're going to steer clear of the content issue—whether what's on TV is good, bad, or indifferent for children, which is a whole other issue—and focus instead on the question of whether television can actually foster concentration and self-regulation. Let's look at the naysayers first.

A leading critic, author Marie Winn (*The Plug-In Drug*), faults television because it permits a child so much intake with so little verbal participation. Winn cites research that shows that television programs do not facilitate lasting verbal development.

What's more, says Winn, studies show that the very act of passive watching does little to help children discover or develop strengths in physical mastery, in social interaction, and in self-regulation, an essential component of focused attention and concentration.

Television robs children of the opportunity to engage in multisensory activities that in the long run will be more intellectually stimulating and more socially and emotionally nourishing. With cardiovascular systems working at their peak and muscles tensed, many children watching television may be passive, but their little bodies are tight and stressed, not relaxed.

> By forming images for children, television may blunt their imaginative abilities.

Television's best skills—sudden close-ups, zoom-ins, bright colors, startling noises—provoke "instinctive responses to danger and excitement" in your child's brain without providing the physical means to relieve them, according to Dr. Thomas Armstrong, an educator of special children. We commonly call this the "fight or flight response." Many experts believe that hyperactivity and irritability in children may be the result of continuous "fight or flight" reactions without activity to provide release. The television watcher neither fights nor runs, but sits and watches, developing a backlash to the body's pent-up need for physical response. Could it be that the five thousand or more hours of watching television that many children have accumulated by the time they are six years old become a lifestyle contributing factor in the increasing number of stress-related disorders doctors now see?

A number of psychological researchers have shown that five- and six-year-old children model the behavior they see on television, engaging in aggressive or violent behavior, mimicking sexually explicit language, or developing nurturing behavior, if that is what they have seen.

In the long run, however, the worst thing television may do for children is form images for them, thereby blunting children's own imaginative abilities, possibly for life. Compare this to the opportunity for children to form their own images—their own inner world—when they are read to, read themselves, or listen to audiotapes of stories. By stimulating their imagination, reading or listening to stories also gives children a greater sense of control. Based on their own experiences, they can make characters look the way they think they should look. After years of participating in the family's Christmas ritual of listening to a recording of Dylan Thomas recite his evocatively descriptive poem, *A Child's Christmas in Wales*, one child we know turned off a televised production of it during the first few minutes. The characters didn't look like those he had created in his mind, and he liked his better.

On the other side of the debate, one of the most outspoken advocates *for* the value of television under certain circumstances is Patricia Marks Greenfield, author of *Mind and Media: The Effects of Television, Video Games, and Computers*. She believes television, video games, and computers are all a means of socialization. Those not watching or playing may be at a social disadvantage among their friends when they talk about various shows and video games. They may need to fit into a peer group by being "hooked" on the same shows as their friends.

So, great: An entire peer group that can't concentrate, as many teachers will testify!

There's even a television commercial showing children at the barbershop talking about their fancy, fast new computer modems and a child who hangs his head as he admits mournfully that his parents still have an older, slower modem. We learn that even the barber's modem is up-to-date, as he kindly reassures the child, "Hey, we all had to start somewhere."

There's something terribly sad about this commercial—as there is, for thoughtful people, about any arguments that place technological or pop cultural imperatives above the importance of a child's physical and mental health. This, too, is a whole other issue, to be sure. When a child's development is at stake, one would hope that adults might realize that there are more important things to worry about than technological snazziness, just as one would

> The good news: If adults carefully mediate television watching, some positive effects may be achieved.

The Benefits of Listening

Educational studies demonstrate that watching television often cannot stimulate the imagination and enhance the ability to concentrate like listening can. When researchers at Yale University set out to evaluate the effects of watching television (*Mr. Rogers' Neighborhood*) on the imaginative play of preschoolers, they found, as might be expected, that a group of children exposed instead to a live adult who gave them exercises and games involving make-believe play and imagination showed the greatest increase in spontaneous imagination and pretend play. Children who watched the show with an adult who mediated the program's imaginative content showed the next greatest gain, while the group that simply watched the show without an adult and a fourth group that watched no television showed no gains in their imaginative play.

In 1980–81 a research organization based at Harvard University, Project Zero, conducted a study to compare the effects of different media on children's comprehension of story mater-

hope that peer pressure would never seem a good enough reason to condone developmentally harmful behavior.

That said, what *about* TV and concentration? Is there any good news here? Well, it does seem possible that if carefully mediated adult participation is added to television watching, some positive effects may be achieved. Children may possibly develop increased abilities in visual–spatial and critical thinking skills, such as comprehending plot, learning about characterization, comprehending thought processes, and understanding what and how individual scenes in a presentation contribute to the whole show. This last element in particular seems an area in which television contributes what reading cannot. There is some

ial. Their findings with regard to television versus reading were both startling and disturbing.

One of the researchers read a children's story (*The Three Robbers* by Tomi Ungerer) from an illustrated storybook to one group of children. A second group viewed a television film of the book, using spoken narration by the same researcher and only the book's illustrations for art.

When tested, the "book children" remembered more of the story and recalled more details when asked to do so than the "television children." They were more likely to remember and use exact words and phrases from the book, while the television children were prone to paraphrasing.

Although both groups tended to reach the same conclusions about the story, those in the televised group relied overwhelmingly on the visual aspects they had seen on the screen to understand the story. In contrast, those who listened to the story used an entirely different reasoning process. They drew on their own personal experiences and their own real-world knowledge for their understanding.

evidence, for instance, that children cannot correctly infer the relationship between scenes until they are around seven or eight years old. Until then, each shot is a separate event for them.

To use television responsibly will without a doubt require some work on your part. By planning your child's or your family's weekly television schedule together, you can help your child develop planning and organizational skills, and sort out values. Dr. Brazelton suggests limiting television viewing to one hour a day during the week and not more than two hours on weekend days. What's more, he suggests that at least half the weekly viewing time should be time in which parents and children watch together. This way, TV becomes a shared family activity, and one in which the family can exchange ideas and discuss the issues, the sports, or the cartoons. Television in general becomes a thoughtful activity this way, rather than a thoughtless one. Exceptional or special programs can become important family events.

And when the television is off, do what parents of the past did. Engage your children in tangible, physical activities. Play games with them, like the ones offered in this book and in *Teaching Your Child Creativity*, or teach them to play games with each other. Help your younger child develop the ability to play alone for extended periods of time—a far more advanced, rewarding skill than the ability to watch TV alone for extended periods of time.

Without the television, children must begin to think for themselves. They must make decisions about what they are going to do; they must locate and participate in things that interest them. They are learning to differentiate what interests them from what doesn't, to persist in exploring or learning about it, and to plan their time—in short, important components of concentration.

CHAPTER NINE

The Role of School

For more than 2,500 years, human cultures have been producing theories about how people learn. In recent decades alone, psychologists have written hundreds of books on the topic. Beginning teachers learn about a variety of these theories in their educational psychology courses.

Needless to say, this is complex stuff. Right away we have to differentiate between a person's learning *style*—that is, his or her particular way of learning—and, underneath it all, how the brain itself "learns" information. Experts have done a lot to explain learning style differences in recent generations. It is widely accepted now that people may differ regarding which sensory input, of five, they favor when it comes to learning.

And so while it's estimated that nearly three-quarters of our knowledge is acquired visually, there are nevertheless children who learn better through their kinesthetic (movement) or tactile (touch) systems or auditory (hearing) systems. We are only recently getting to the point at which our educational system is understanding this and doing a better job at fitting the teaching method to the child's favored modality—or, better yet, using all three to be sure that every child gets the information imparted.

Around 65 percent of us in the United States are visual learners who concentrate on and learn best from written information, diagrams, and pictures. These are, of course, the customary materials to which children are exposed in most classrooms. Visual learners are usually unhappy and do not do well if they have to acquire their knowledge by listening and are not allowed to take detailed notes. Children who are visually oriented learn to read best through word recognition.

Auditory learners, on the other hand, learn to read through hearing differences between sounds, and relate best to the spoken word. Comprising about 30 percent of the population, they like to listen first and take notes afterward, if at all, or to rely later on printed notes.

Only about 5 percent of us are kinesthetic/tactile learners, although there may be more among younger children. These children learn most effectively through touch and movement through space, and many hyperactive children learn better when allowed to move. Kinesthetic learners are exceptionally good at learning skills by imitation and practice. When material to be learned is not presented in their style, they may appear to be slow learners. They may learn to read best, for instance, by tracing letters in the sand or by creating words using letters cut from sandpaper and identifying them only by touch.

Underneath an individual's learning style, however, there are believed to be basic physiological and neurological commonalities to how the brain works to learn. We have seen in earlier chapters how the infant first learns about her world simply by looking at things that are novel. Her attention is easily interrupted as sensory input changes. Gradually, as neurological development occurs, she can attend to input from several senses simultaneously. She can hold a toy and listen to music at the same time without dropping the toy. This is the next "baby step" in her developing attention span.

As her motor and perceptual skills improve, she begins to "pay attention" to more complicated input, especially that which requires a movement or physical response from her, and she can concentrate on it to the exclusion of all other incoming information. With progressive maturation, the period of time during which she can concentrate on a task that involves more than one stimuli, or incoming piece of information, and not be distracted by insignificant or inconsequential stimuli steadily increases. Deliberate learning/teaching is now possible, but what exactly is that?

> Schools must become better at understanding differences in learning style and temperament.

Well, as it turns out, this is what becomes unclear. For all of our hundreds, even thousands, of years of theorizing, we still don't have a satisfactory explanation for how, exactly, specifically we learn things. Today, experts believe we fall short because we do not know enough about the brain and nervous system. In the past, there have been other explanations; in the future, perhaps, still more. The bottom line is, human consciousness is still a pretty mysterious phenomenon.

Still, we try to understand it. When it comes to learning, experts have boiled it down to two primary ideas relating to how the brain appears to make connections that extend what has been previously learned. The first is called association, or stimulus-response learning. This involves the fairly mechanical idea of connecting information already stored in the brain to incoming information, leading to a new learned skill or idea. For instance, a baby cries, is picked up, and is comforted. The same thing happens the next time she cries. The third time she cries, it is not because she is hungry or wet, but because she simply wants to be comforted again. She has "learned" how to receive comfort.

A second theory of learning, sometimes called the "a-ha" theory, or the cognitive theory, applies especially to problem-solving. This theory says that a child's behavior does not necessarily have to follow a trial-and-error pattern of learning, but may develop through a rather sudden and complete under-standing—an insight—of how to solve a problem. Pretty mysterious, still.

Either of these techniques leads to developing memory, although some theorists believe that memory is not merely the form of learning in itself.

Memory is typically divided into short term and long term. Short-term memory occurs for seconds or sometimes minutes. We look up a telephone number, remember it, and make our call. By the time the conversation is finished, we have forgotten the number. Long-term memory can last long enough to take an examination or, depending on its importance, for a lifetime. Repetition and rehearsing (what most of us call memorization) can help transfer short-term memory to long term. What we think of as memory are actually chemical changes—scientists call them "memory traces"—that are stored in the neurons (nerve cells) in different areas of the brain, depending on whether the memory is short term, long term, language memories, numerical memories, etc.

While the development of modern technology now permits us to image what parts of the brain are active during certain memory tasks, we still don't know exactly where memory takes place and how it is stored. One thing experts are clear on, however, is that we do not remember everything we have ever learned or experienced. If this were true, the mind would be a storehouse of miscellaneous, unsorted data. Information can be lost through disuse or become flawed through intense emotion or reinterpretation.

Memory versus Learning

Whatever memory actually is and however it takes place, one thing that has become clearer to experts in recent years is the difference, in traditional school environments, between goading students to memorize facts and a knowing focus on helping children learn to concentrate better.

Memory and memorization are important, to be sure. But too much lecturing and questioning, with little regard either to self-selection of content or to learning style differences, may prompt students to remember things without any improved ability to concentrate. Teachers who admonish children to "pay attention" seem to think children already have concentration skills built in, or will develop them simply as a result of their scolding.

More and more experts today urge for greater understanding within our educational system of differences in both learning styles and temperaments that exist among children. Teachers unskilled in this area are prone to evaluate certain behavior as "resistant," "uncooperative," or "needs to follow instructions better," when, in fact, if a child is given different instructions, allowed to learn differently, or given advance warning about when an activity must end, negative behavior disappears.

Research conducted at UCLA and other universities found that too often teachers' judgments of a child's actual learning abilities and teachability were based on what were, in fact, variations in temperamental patterns. Further, many, perhaps most, teachers are not trained in individualized instruction despite the fact that research also shows that group instruction is far less effective.

Predating, and yet responding to, all of these educational complaints was an important educational figure of the late nineteenth century, Maria Montessori. An Italian medical doctor, she became interested in education originally through her efforts to teach mentally disabled children. Montessori successfully adapted and developed an educational technique and special teaching materials based on the work that two French researchers, Jean Itard and Edouard Séguin, had accomplished with deaf and "subnormal" children.

> Parents can evaluate how a school develops children's abilities to concentrate.

Following her success with mentally disabled children, Montessori turned her attention to children who came from underprivileged families. Establishing a school for them, she found that her approach was successful with these children as well. Today, Montessori schools can be found throughout the United States and in more than fifty countries on six continents. Montessori has sometimes been referred to as the "spiritual mother" of programs such as Head Start.

Although Montessori's work constitutes just one approach to learning, it is important in general because its child-centered approach is firmly grounded in the developmental stages of children, and keeps in mind the notion that a child's education must be viewed in its entirety, not one year at a time; her efforts are significant within the context of our discussion here because her methods appear at once to promote both concentration and long-term educational success. Admittedly, no single approach works equally well for every child, but Montessori's successes offer us insight into learning and development in general.

Montessori believed that at each period in development, there were specific "sensitivities" that facilitated reaching definitive goals of that period. At each stage interest and learning begin slowly, reach a peak, and then decline when the goals are achieved. This contrasts with the linear education of public schools, where education follows a steady ascent, becoming increasingly more difficult with each year.

Oriented toward long-range goals, Montessori education allows each child to progress at his or her own pace toward developmental goals by building on one skill after another. That one stage may take longer for one child than it does for another does not constitute a problem; hence, you have a classroom full of children working at different levels with different materials in a specially "prepared" environment. Montessori education is based on the philosophy that children's learning will become exciting to them in direct proportion to the extent that they are allowed to discover solutions for themselves.

A series of Canadian research studies with hyperactive children conducted by Dr. Donald Sykes demonstrated that, in tasks in which the child is in control of the situation and able to pace herself, she performs the same as other children, but when the experimenter controls the task, she does worse.

Montessori believed that when a teacher tells children what they should explore, how to do so, and what they are to discover, their interest and behavior steadily deteriorate. They lose their enthusiasm for learning and become dependent upon adult monitoring and control.

Now, certainly, the Montessori method is not the only approach to learning and concentration; succesful methods have been used in public, private, and parochial schools. But one of the noticeable things about Montessori children is that because of the way they are educated, they are accustomed to accepting responsibility and to initiating and completing work independent of teacher direction. By the end of their six years in an elementary Montessori schoolroom, graduates have—or surpass—the academic skills and knowledge of children in the regular school system. Because of the way they have learned, they typically have greater confidence, self-regulation, and ability to concentrate—more mature learning skills—than their public school peers. In 1978 a group of American parents established the first middle school (ages twelve through fifteen) based on Montessori principles. Now there are more than one hundred in the United States, and their number continues to grow.

The Rhythms of Learning

A number of years ago, a popular fad encouraged people to become aware of their biorhythms. People bought electronic gadgets to alert themselves to good days—when they would be most effective—and "critical days," when they would be prone to accidents.

But, fads aside, it is true that our internal rhythms affect our learning skills and our attention span. There is even an entire field of science—chronopsychology—that studies the effects of our various biological rhythms on our physical, mental, and emotional capacities. Because of the twenty-four–hour rhythmic cycle that we all experience, most of us—except for "night owls"—are more alert in the morning.

Beginning around noon, our attention begins to decline and continues to do so throughout the afternoon. Doesn't it make sense, then, that many children might be better off doing their homework in the morning?

We are better at problem-solving in the morning, and our short-term memory works best around 9 AM. This is the part of the day when teachers should schedule tests, drills, lectures— any topic to which a child must pay close attention. When long-term memory is stronger—near 3 PM—it's time to introduce

What to Look for in a School

For the most part, teachers in our public schools are unable to structure their classes so that each child can pace herself and learn with her own timing. This is often not the fault of the teacher, who must conform to school standards and state regulations and must pass the child onto another teacher at the end of the academic year.

Still, there are things that you, as a parent, can look for in your child's classroom to indicate that the school is at least

interesting and stimulating activities in which movement is allowed.

Throughout the day we have 90- to 120-minute rhythms, which psychologist Ernest Rossi calls the ultradian rhythm. This natural rhythm constitutes a shift from activity to rest, or to right-hemispheric dominance. It means that in daily life we usually need to take a break every hour and a half or so. Ultradian rhythms are the biological basis for those times when we find ourselves daydreaming. Dr. Rossi calls them "normal periods of turning inward." We need them for emotional and physiological balance.

However, it is not clear how accurately the ultradian rhythm applies to children, for Dr. Montessori found that when children become self-directed and are pacing their own learning, they do best when allowed a three-hour uninterrupted work cycle.

Check out your daily rhythms for yourself. Keep a diary of when you and your child perform better on certain activities, how long you can work at certain activities, and when you need to take a break after continuous activity. Check out your child's school. Learn when various activities are scheduled to determine if the school is "with the rhythm" or forcing your child to fit.

attempting to promote self-pacing and developing your child's
ability to concentrate:

☆ Check if there is time allotted and equipment available,
such as at a science center, where children have the opportunity to pursue some of their learning at their own pace.
Must they only engage in specified projects at learning
centers, or are they, at least sometimes, free to follow
their own interests?

☆ Does the teacher provide a variety of sensory material for
visual, kinesthetic, tactile, and auditory learning? Does
he allow or encourage children in their own styles of
learning, or does he require all children to learn the same
way? Do all children, or groups of children, have to be
doing the same thing at the same time?

☆ Does the teacher allow your child to follow her own
interests and tie them into the regular curricula? You may
need actively to enlist the teacher's cooperation, and sup-
port her efforts, in providing the best learning opportunities for your child so that knowledge and concentration
can develop hand-in-hand.

☆ Arrange a meeting with the principal to find out her ideas
on how children learn to concentrate, how she thinks
they not only increase their attention span, but also
develop accompanying motivation—or if she thinks these
two are even tied together. How does the principal apply
her philosophy to the school's teachers; that is, must they
all abide by it, or are they free to help children develop
concentrational skills based on their own philosophies?

CHAPTER TEN

Concentration- Related Learning Disabilities

American parents haven't been quite the same since *Why Johnny Can't Concentrate*, by Dr. Robert A. Moss, hit the bookstores in 1990. After decades of society's wrestling with certain types of overactive, hard-to-control children, Moss gathered everything under what was, for most of us, a new umbrella: Attention Deficit Disorder (ADD). Moss hadn't invented the term—he wasn't even completely happy with it—but he nevertheless put it out there for the general public like no one had before.

No two children with ADD are alike, Moss said. They may exhibit a number of disconcerting behaviors, such as distractibility, poor organizational ability, impulsivity, free flight of ideas, difficulty feeling satisfied, high activity level, social immaturity, mood swings, performance inconsistency, and memory dysfunction.

The behavior of ADD children may vary from day to day, and according to Moss, their most consistent attribute is their inconsistency. For many the decision of whether to label a child as one with ADD is fraught with potential for error. But to parents, Moss's book was invaluable in alerting them to the notion that none of these behaviors their child was exhibiting was intentional or malicious, and in bringing to the forefront, once again, behaviors that society had been trying to classify—and therefore contain—for most of this century.

The ADD "industry" has blossomed ever since. Moss's book, however, was not the first to focus attention on children who can't seem to pay attention. Before there was ADD, there was hyperactivity (now, of course, the two are often combined in what some call AD/HD: Attention Deficit/Hyperactivity Disorder). A pioneering book in this area was *The Myth of the Hyperactive Child and Other Means of Child Control*, written in 1975 but largely ignored today. In it, co-authors Peter Schrag and Diane Divoky penned a scathing attack on the decisions of authorities responsible for the education and socialization to "honor every annoying habit of childhood" with a "pseudo-scientific designation." Schools, doctors, and juvenile authorities, drawing on medical evidence that a small percentage of our youthful population suffers from brain damage, had begun to attribute similar ailments to "millions of children who suffer from no scientifically demonstrable ailments but whose behavior is regarded as troublesome to adults," wrote the authors. An unnamed California psychiatrist told the authors, simply and emphatically, that "a hyperactive child is a pre-delinquent child."

Whether called hyperactivity, ADD, or something else in another few years, this whole idea of labeling behavior is an extraordinarily tricky business. One of the problems of defining and diagnosing ADD is the very fact that children comprising this group *are* so widely diverse and likely to differ in symptoms, intelligence, and styles of learning. Another problem is that at least a few of the behavioral characteristics in question are present, to one extent or another, in almost every child at some point in his or her development.

A more recent book that sheds light on the issue is Thomas Armstrong's *The Myth of the ADD Child*, published in 1995. A child psychologist and former special education teacher, Armstrong, echoing some of the ideas first presented by Schrag and Divoky, thinks of ADD as a myth because information about it represents a "coherently organized system of beliefs" that gives little attention to the "broader social, political, economic, psychological, and educational issues" that surround the term.

> American children are twenty times more likely than children in other countries to be diagnosed with ADD.

According to Armstrong, substantial evidence suggests that although children labeled as ADD sufferers may behave in certain ways in a traditional classroom, they often do not show symptoms of the disorder in several different real-life contexts—namely, in one-on-one situations (especially with their fathers); in classrooms in which they are allowed to choose their activities and set their own pace; during activities when their motivational level is high because they are paid; and when involved in situations that interest them, are novel in some way, or involve high levels of stimulation.

What's more, notes Armstrong, when about half the diagnosed children reach adulthood, ADD just disappears, although there is as much controversy about whether or not this is true as there is about other characteristics of ADD. For instance, Moss thinks that the disorder doesn't disappear but rather that by the time they reach adulthood, ADD children have learned to compensate such that their learning difficulty is no longer a major disability. One doctor estimates that attention deficits remain in 60 percent of adults diagnosed as children.

Armstrong doesn't deny that the behaviors exist, but insists that they are not a medical disorder but rather more complex and multifaceted. "Ultimately," he writes, "there may be as many explanations for ADD behavior as there are children with the label."

Indictments and questions notwithstanding, the prevailing notion remains that ADD is in fact neurologically based, possibly of genetic origin, and that it affects from 3 percent (for girls) to 10 percent (for boys) of American children (although earlier quasi-official estimates put the number closer to 40 percent).

Historically, ADD was first officially noticed in the early part of the twentieth century when Dr. George Frederic Still, lecturing to the Royal College of Physicians in England, described some twenty children in his clinical practice whose behavior indicated they shared a "basic defect in moral control." It was downhill from there. In the 1970s psychiatrist Camilla M. Anderson suggested that children with minimal brain damage should be kept from "breeding."

Since that time similar behaviors to those described by Moss have been categorized by as many as twenty-five different names, including organic drivenness, restless syndrome, postencephalitic behavior disorder, hyperkinetic reaction of childhood, developmental hyperactivity, and Strauss syndrome. For a while in the 1950s and 1960s, this behavior was deemed the result of minimal brain damage and children were designated as having minimal brain dysfunction. It was definitely a disorder in search of a name.

Then in 1980 the American Psychiatric Association listed attention deficit disorder in the third edition of its *Diagnostic and Statistical Manual of Mental Disorders (DSM III)*, officially making it a "disease," even if not too many people were, well, paying attention at the time. In 1987, when the manual was revised, the name of the disorder was changed to Attention Deficit/Hyperactivity Disorder (AD/HD), despite the fact that many children labeled with attention deficit are not hyperactive. When the manual was once again revised in 1994, the term AD/HD came to distinguish between behavior in which six or more characteristics of *inattention* have been the predominant characteristic for at least six months, and behavior in

Strengths of Children with ADD

ADD may not be a totally negative experience; like all children, those diagnosed with ADD have some particularly positive attributes.

Even though they may be having trouble with schoolwork, numerous research studies have established that children with ADD are usually as smart as, and often smarter than, other children their age. They are also extremely creative and innovative, and often artistically talented.

Children with ADD have a unique perspective. Frequently they view the world quite differently from their peers and parents, providing unusual and rewarding insights if you are open to them. They have an inordinate amount of curiosity and knack for experimentation, which is sometimes a blessing, and sometimes scary. For instance, a few of the "fun" things Nancy Boyles and Darlene Contadino have learned from their children with ADD include the facts that tennis shoes don't leak pancake syrup, peanut-butter bread sticks to the ceiling, and no matter how many eggs you crack open on the living room rug, they will all have the yellow things in the middle of them.

Problem-solvers learn from their own experience. ADD children bravely go where few have gone before in their persistent quest to concentrate on finding the answers to questions that puzzle them.

which *hyperactivity-impulsivity* is the distinguishing character-istic. When the three major characteristics of ADD—inatten-tion, hyperactivity, and impulsivity—are all present, the category becomes AD/HD, combined type. Now you know.

> The problem is not that the ADD child doesn't pay atten-tion, but that he is paying attention to everything.

While more than 95 percent of indi-viduals with ADD have been shown not to have any brain damage, one of the early theories behind the disorder was that persons with ADD had a shortage of neurotransmitters, probably inher-ited from their father. Neurotransmit-ters are chemicals that carry messages from one brain cell to the next. When we concentrate, our brain releases extra neuro-transmitters, causing the "switch on" signals to travel more quickly, enabling us to focus more on one area or topic and to block out competing stimuli. The theory that fewer neurotrans-mitters were the basis for ADD developed in a backward way—it was found that giving a hyperactive child with ADD a stimulant (Ritalin) paradoxically slows down the hyperactive behavior. Therefore, doctors postulated that the medication increased the production of neurotransmitters. Recent genetic research has strengthened the idea that such a link may exist.

Most recently, a 1996 study funded by the National Institute of Mental Health suggests that the inability to focus may be, in fact, the result of subtle structural abnormalities in those parts of the brain that inhibit thoughts. Magnetic resonance imaging of the brains of fifty-seven boys, ages five to eighteen, who had difficulty staying focused showed their brains were more sym-metrical than those of fifty-five age-matched controls. Nor-mally the right side of the brain is larger than the left.

More specifically, the symmetry resulted in a smaller-than-normal size of three of the structures located on the right side of the brain, including an area believed to serve as the brain's command center (the prefrontal) as well as the area thought to be responsible for translating neurological commands into action (known as the globus pallidus).

In *Parenting a Child with Attention Deficit/Hyperactivity Disorder*, the most up-to-date book written for parents, authors Nancy S. Boyles, an educator, and Darlene Contadino, a social worker—both of whom have children with ADD—say that ADD is rarely found in isolation. Other disorders often accompany ADD, including "learning disabilities, Tourette's syndrome, language processing disabilities, sensory integration issues, obsessive-compulsive disorder, mood disorders, oppositional defiant disorder, and conduct disorder." On the one hand, this is interesting; on the other hand, it doesn't tell us very much, since each of these disorders is also seen in isolation with sufficient frequency to assure that none is simply a by-product of the other. And so the precise nature of their relationship to one another remains—as do many things up there in the brain—a mystery.

Characteristics of ADD

One indisputable characteristic of children with ADD, of course, is the trouble they have concentrating. This not only dismays and frustrates teachers and parents, it also upsets the children too—especially if their behavior is erroneously believed to be deliberate, uncaring, or in defiance of authority. It's often hard for parents and teachers to think otherwise, especially when this behavior is compared to that of peers with developmentally appropriate attention spans. And yet one of the greatest services to the child you can perform as parent or teacher is to recognize that he is not acting this way on purpose.

A common misconception of the child or person with ADD, often furthered by the school situation, is that he doesn't or won't pay attention. Not only is this wrong, but it's counterproductive to make this assumption, since at least part of the problem is that the child is, in fact, paying attention to everything. This makes him either easily distracted from the task at hand or overwhelmed by all the incoming information. Or both. You see, the ADD child responds to every action around him, every instruction, and to all that's going on in his mind, and has difficulty comprehending the importance or priority of any of it. He may be so overwhelmed with all this input that he hears only bits and pieces of the teacher's instructions, as his attention shifts again and again.

He is slow to action and has difficulty following routines or completing tasks without supervision. He also has trouble following rules, and is as distractible in social situations as when he is at home or at school, i.e., he often doesn't appear to be listening or may forget promises to friends. He constantly loses possessions. Academically, his performance is inconsistent: sometimes it is high, sometimes very low—leading teachers to notice that he frequently "fails to live up to his potential." He has trouble taking notes and organizing not only school assignments but everything around him. His locker, his desk, and his bedroom are all a mess.

Ritalin Reality

One important issue tied up with the complex debate on concentration-related learning disabilities is, of course, the administering of drugs as treatment. Since the 1960s, Ritalin (methylphenidate hydrochloride), an amphetamine-like drug, has been the first choice for controlling the hyperactivity of ADD-diagnosed children in the United States, although physicians have also prescribed other amphetamines, tranquilizers, antidepressants, anticonvulsants, and even antipsychotic medications. In truth, Ritalin was never supposed to be the only form of intervention for ADD children, but rather it was intended to calm them down enough that it could be used in conjunction with nondrug measures. All too often, however, it is relied on as the only form of treatment.

So children taking Ritalin calm down, but at what cost? If your child has ADD, only you can decide if the results are worth it. Some children appear to cry more easily than before, and to become less creative and innovative. The most common side effects are nervousness, jitteriness, and insomnia. Other well-known reactions include decreased appetite, stomachache, nausea, headache, dizziness, drowsiness, tachycardia (rapid heartbeat), depressed affect, and sadness. All are supposed to be minimal and relieved with dosage adjustment, but, of course, as with all medications, that depends on the person taking it. Until the right dosage is arrived at, there may be some uncomfortable times. In rare cases, Ritalin has triggered seizures, Tourette's syndrome, and glaucoma. It is not advised for children under six years old, and—this is absolutely crucial to understand—*no information exists on the safety and efficacy of long-term use.*

The fact that it is addictive is also usually not discussed. The *Physicians' Desk Reference* refers to it as a "mild central nervous system stimulant." In fact, Ritalin is classified as a Schedule II drug by the Drug Enforcement Administration, which means that among all legal drugs, it ranks right up there with morphine and barbiturates in having a high potential for abuse.

According to educator Thomas Armstrong, one of the assumptions many make about the need for Ritalin is that children learn best if they keep still, when, in fact, Armstrong's experience shows that some children need to hear music playing in order to learn, while others need to be able to move around in order to concentrate. Or, they may need to break up their study time with frequent movement breaks.

While the usual response toward hyperactive children is to shut down or control the amount of information that is incoming, one special education researcher, Sydney Zentall, found that when hyperactive children were put in a room that contained brightly colored pictures, posters and rugs, strings of brightly lit Christmas lights, a cage of mice, and rock music playing in the background, they were able to calm down and complete an academic task as well as when they were in a less stimulating room. Zentall speculated that home and school environments may not be meeting the needs of hyperactive children for exciting, novel, and stimulating learning experiences. Other studies confirm that hyperactive children do not like to continue in repetitive tasks.

Other research studies have shown that when children rated as hyperactive were observed in an "open" classroom, their amount of observable activity did not differ from that of a control group of so-called "normal" children, whereas in the confined setting of a more formal or "closed" classroom, the control-group children became considerably more passive.

If a child can be optimally stimulated, he may not need psychostimulants such as Ritalin, according to Armstrong. Could we be using psychostimulants to help children adjust to what Dr. Armstrong calls "boring, routine-ridden, repetition-plagued classrooms," rather than spending the time and money to enrich the educational environment? Psychiatrists Stella Chess and Alexander Thomas caution against the carelessness of labeling a child hyperactive who is in fact merely restless and fidgety in a boring classroom with a dull, unstimulating teacher who finds the child a "nuisance."

Whatever you believe about the causes and consequences of ADD, it is now considered a disability under federal law because it can substantially limit a major life activity such as learning or working. Individuals with ADD are guaranteed free and appropriate public education by three federal laws: Section 504 of the Rehabilitation Act (RA, 1973), the Americans with Disabilities Act (ADA, 1990), and the Individuals with Disabilities Education Act (IDEA, 1990). After a student is found eligible, the school system must put together a team consisting of parents, the student, teachers, specialists, and a representative of the public agency qualified to provide special services in order to design an individualized educational program (IEP) or an Accommodation Plan (depending on which law the student qualifies under) to meet the student's unique needs.

What Do You Do?

In the face of all these conflicting scientific theories, many parents are at a loss when they believe their child shows certain symptoms of ADD. The most important question remains: What are parents to do if their child appears to have a concentration-related learning disability?

In short, two steps are essential to take in answering this question. First, review all the facts, and have in-depth discussions with your child's teachers and school counselors. Then, speak to qualified professionals to chart a proper course of action.

CHAPTER ELEVEN

Concentration and Potential

If you've learned anything about concentration by now (and we do hope you have!), you might want to concentrate now on this one, emergent idea: Concentration involves, or is related to, a number of important skills that are also the hallmarks of successful people. This is no coincidence.

It begins with curiosity, and develops as the child learns what she likes or what unknown topic (that is to say, "toy") holds her interest. By the time a child is two years old, her brain has developed sufficiently so that she can generate an idea, select the tools or objects she needs, and implement a plan, albeit a simple one, with a resistance to distraction that would make the most dedicated executive proud.

Increasingly she becomes able to remember more objects and to understand ideas and concepts. With growing maturity, she learns to connect past knowledge with present activity (memory), and to contain natural human anxiety or tension—which difficult or new problems generate—long enough to gather sufficient information that might be useful in solving such problems.

155

Jerome Kagan tells us that the "key tension" in every problem is that our first choice is to use knowledge and abilities that have worked in the past, but part of us is concurrently aware that our old ways may not be adequate to the new task and

> The ability to concentrate greatly increases a child's chances for a life of joy and purpose.

must be altered. We have to be able to "hang in there," to persevere, long enough to overcome this tension. Our children learn this bit by bit if allowed plenty of time and age-appropriate stimulation. Concentration—what may have originally seemed like such a simple concept—gradually evolves via all these developmental tasks.

As your child grows, one of the most important and effective ways you can help her develop concentrational skills is to model these skills yourself. Children who perceive a parent as being able to concentrate, or engaging in persistent efforts to complete a task—possibly returning to various elements of the task again and again with more skill—will identify with that parent and come to regard it as important that they, too, develop similar skills. They will learn that concentration is valued in their home.

Start with being aware of subtle messages you send through casual comments. For instance, you might try, if you can, to remove the sentence "Hurry up and finish" from your vocabulary. Concentration is much more likely to be promoted by a statement such as "You can come back to it after dinner." If children learn that you expect them to finish, or to continue to pursue a project, and that you will provide the time to do so— both for yourself and for them—they come to expect to have success at concentrating. And success arrives. Your child learns what you already know and so aptly demonstrate: concentration and success are partners.

If you are a parent who pursues your own interests or hobbies in your spare time, rather than sitting in front of the television, your child will also discover that there are more rewarding things to do—activities that are not only acceptable but also gratifying and fun.

If you are a parent who regularly takes time to explore new and unusual events and activities, your child also comes to know that there are interesting topics to learn more about and better ways to learn than from the television—although it is possible that certain television shows may spark just such an interest, if the interest is followed up with real-life activity.

One bright child we know had a mother who encouraged exploration of varied interests, and who exposed her children to cultural events and arranged museum visits. Once when the child went to her mother to ask about a particular subject, the mother responded, "I don't know." "Don't you *want* to know?" was the child's immediate response, and the mother and child began to learn together. Show your children there is all the time they need to find out what they want to know. It will pay off in the future.

As adults, concentration helps us lead rich lives by allowing us to engage in a number of work and recreational activities that are pleasurable in their pursuit and eminently satisfying in their accomplishment. Little wonder that philosophers through the ages have paid almost mystical reverence to concentration. Adults who can concentrate are far more likely to lead lives of joy and purpose than those whose minds flutter from one thought to another, whose activities are infrequently completed, and whose goals are scarcely realized. It may well be that concentration is one of the most important abilities that distinguishes happiness from boredom.

Think about it....

Index